THE FEEDBACK EFFECT

Lead Smarter, Not Harder With the Science of Human Behavior

DR. PAUL GAVONI

Heart & Science International, LLC
heartscienceinternational.org

THE
FEEDBACK
EFFECT

This book is a work of nonfiction. Unless otherwise noted, the authors and publisher make no explicit guarantees as to the accuracy of the information contained in this book, and in some cases, the names of people and places have been altered to protect their privacy. This book reflects the authors' original ideas and insights, alongside those of cited sources. Artificial intelligence was utilized solely to refine the reading experience, ensuring clarity and accessibility while preserving the authenticity of the content. This book is intended to provide a simple introduction to behavior analysis that will be readily understood by members of the general public. The content features limited inclusion of technical terminology and simplified coverage of technical notions.

Authors: Paul Gavoni and Adam Ventura

The Feedback Effect: *Lead Smarter, Not Harder With the Science of Human Behavior*

Published by: Heart & Science Consulting, LLC

Publisher: Paul Gavoni

ISBN: 978-1-7359034-7-7 (Paperback)
ISBN: 978-1-7359034-8-4 (Hardback)
ISBN: 978-1-7359034-9-1 (eBook)

Paulie's Dedication

For Jeremy D. Meduri (1988–2025)

Gone too soon.

As I was finishing this book, I received the heartbreaking news that one of my clients, Jeremy Meduri, had passed. He was just 37.

Jeremy was a kind soul who genuinely wanted to make a difference in the world. I still remember when he first reached out to bring me in for a keynote. He shared that he used to jog while listening to my podcast and, during tough moments at work, would ask himself, *"What would Paulie say or do?"* That level of respect was deeply humbling.

Some of the struggles Jeremy was facing reminded me of my younger self—fighting to do good, trying to make things better, but feeling the weight of it all. Maybe that's why I connected with him so quickly. I found myself rooting for him. And I truly believe that if we had lived closer, we would've been close friends.

His passing hit me hard. I broke down in tears. So young. So full of life. So determined to do good.

This book is dedicated to Jeremy—his heart, his hope, and the difference he made while he was here. May his story remind us all to look out for each other, and to keep doing the work that matters.

—Paulie

PREFACE

When Feedback Fails

A few years ago, on short notice, I was asked to observe an employee. Their supervisor had concerns and wanted a second set of eyes. I agreed to observe, then stopped in quickly before heading to a conference. I didn't introduce myself. I didn't explain why I was there. I simply sat off to the side and took notes while the person worked.

To be fair, I tried to balance my observations—acknowledging what was going well and offering feedback on what needed improvement. I later emailed the employee a summary of my thoughts, wrapped it up with kind words, and left for my flight.

The next day, I opened my inbox to find a response:

"Your rhetoric falls on deaf ears."

That was it. No greeting, no closing—just one sentence that landed harder than anything I'd written. And it stung. Because it was true.

Without context, consent, or relationship, my feedback felt invasive and condescending. It didn't matter how accurate my analysis was. The delivery undermined the message.

In another situation, I wasn't consulting—I was a leader within the organization. A team member was underperforming, and it was affecting others. But I liked this person. I wanted to preserve the relationship. So, I leaned heavily on praise. I offered encouragement. I gave them space and recognition for what was going well.

What I didn't do? Deliver honest, necessary correction.

And the cost was steep.

Performance declined. Team frustration grew. The culture took a hit. All because I avoided a conversation I should've had early and clearly. I told myself I was protecting the relationship, but in truth, I was protecting myself from discomfort—and let the team down in the process.

When we don't deliver the right feedback the right way, performance suffers. So do relationships.

The lessons that shaped this book came from direct experience—moments where behavior didn't shift, outcomes suffered, or trust eroded due to missing or ineffective feedback. What emerged was a clear pattern: performance improves when behavior is consistently shaped by meaningful consequences.

This book is about making that process intentional.

It gives leaders actionable strategies grounded in behavioral science to deliver feedback that builds trust, strengthens performance, and supports long-term growth.

Now let's get into it.

TABLE OF CONTENTS

ACKNOWLEDGMENTS

Thank you to my son, Niko Gavoni, for offering clear, thoughtful feedback that made a meaningful impact on this book. Your attention to detail and support helped elevate the quality of the final product.

Gratitude to Sorah Cheryl Eyrich, Stephanie Waldon of Phoenix Rising ABA, and Kyra Brown for your valuable input during the editing process. Your careful review and suggestions directly contributed to the clarity, flow, and overall behavioral precision of this work. Your involvement brought real value, and I'm grateful for the time and care you invested.

A heartfelt thank you to Leb *(www.lebanonraingam.com)*, my trusted formatter for all of my self-published books. You've consistently delivered with precision and reliability—even in those last-minute crunch moments. I'm grateful for your calm under pressure and the vital role you play in bringing these projects to life.

ACKNOWLEDGMENTS

INTRODUCTION

Feedback is one of the most overlooked, misunderstood, and under-leveraged tools in a leader's toolbox. In fact, a Gallup study found that only 26% of employees strongly agree the feedback they receive helps them do better work (Gallup, 2019). That's a problem. Without useful feedback, performance stalls, errors go uncorrected, and potential remains untapped.

More recently, Gallup and Workhuman (2023) found that employees who receive frequent, high-quality feedback paired with recognition are significantly more engaged, less likely to experience burnout, and less likely to be looking for a new job. Still, most workplaces continually fall short.

Most leadership books validate the importance of feedback. They talk about the "art" of it—delivering it with tact, empathy, and charisma. They offer checklists for how to phrase it, when to give it, and how to soften the blow.

And yet, something's missing.

While well-intended, many of these approaches ignore the science of human behavior. They promote strategies that sound good but lack the precision needed to consistently change behavior. They overlook the basic truth that feedback isn't just a leadership skill—it's a behavioral tool. And because all outcomes in organizations are produced by behavior, any tool that shapes, sustains, or redirects behavior—like feedback—is fundamentally a behavioral tool. When we fail to understand the science behind it, we leave growth, improvement, and culture to chance. Performance feedback, as defined in this book, means providing information about specific behaviors and their results, measured against clear and observable criteria or standards.

As a former boxer turned MMA coach, the fight game has taken me all over the world—from Italy and the UK to Russia, where one of my fighters became heavyweight champion of the world. On television, you might catch a glimpse of me in the corner yelling, "Circle out!" "Level change!" or "Watch the right!"—those sharp, in-the-moment cues that can make the difference between victory and defeat. But what most people don't see is that the feedback starts long before the fight itself.

It starts in the gym. In the drills. In the subtle nod when a fighter corrects their footwork, or the brief pause to course-correct when they're getting sloppy on the pads. That's where the loop is built—where feedback becomes familiar, expected, and effective. By the time we hit fight night, we move beyond teaching to prompting and shaping performance in real time.

Leadership is no different. If we wait until people are "in the ring" to offer feedback, we're too late. The best leaders, like the best coaches, build fluent feedback systems long before the pressure hits. Whether it's a title shot or a team deadline—performance rises or falls on the quality of feedback.

This next section lays out the underlying science of human behavior. For some, that might sound a little intimidating—but I encourage you to give it a shot. While the science can run deep—with over a century of research, thousands of studies, and entire volumes dedicated to it—I've worked hard to boil it down to the bare essence. Not to oversimplify, but to make it useful. My goal here isn't to impress you with jargon. It's to help you understand the "why" behind the strategies you'll see in the chapters ahead. Once you understand what actually drives behavior, you'll start seeing problems more clearly, intervening more precisely, and leading more effectively.

You don't need a PhD in behavior analysis to lead effectively, but you do need a working understanding of how behavior works. That's what this section is for. Behavior is the engine. Let's talk about what drives it.

BEHAVIOR IS THE ENGINE

All results in an organization require behavior—whether it's hitting sales targets, improving instruction, reducing errors, or strengthening collaboration. If behavior is the engine of results, feedback is the steering wheel. It's how we influence direction, accelerate progress, and avoid costly detours. That's why leaders need more than intuition—they need behavioral precision.

The science of human behavior is not random—it's rooted in evolutionary principles. Just as physical traits are selected across generations to improve a species' chances of survival and reproduction, **behaviors are selected by their consequences**. In short, we do what we do because of what happens as a result. Organisms—including humans—allocate behavior across milliseconds, minutes, and months toward outcomes that matter. These outcomes fall into two categories: **proximate causes**, which are tied to immediate consequences, and

ultimate causes, which are tied to longer-term consequences that promote thriving over time.

Take the cheetah. Its speed wasn't selected by committee—it was selected by the environment. Faster cheetahs caught more prey, survived longer, and passed on their genes. Those consequences are the **ultimate cause** of the behavior. But in the moment, what gets the cheetah to sprint? The sight of prey, the feeling of hunger, and the opportunity to feed—**proximate causes**. Short-term consequences initiate the behavior; long-term consequences maintain and shape it across generations.

The same process plays out in the workplace every day. A manager sends a Slack message reminding an employee about an upcoming deadline—that's an **antecedent**, a prompt. The employee shifts their focus and begins preparing the report—**behavior**. After submitting it, the manager replies, "Thanks for jumping on this—your summary made the meeting run smoother"—**consequence**. That consequence, positive feedback, increases the likelihood the behavior will happen again.

But none of this occurs in a vacuum. Behavior is also influenced by what behavior scientists call a **motivating operation**, or **MO**. A simple example? When you haven't had anything to drink in a while, water becomes more valuable—and the likelihood of you drinking it increases. You don't need someone to tell you it's good for you. Your body creates the motivation. That's a motivating operation at work.

In behavioral terms, an MO is anything that temporarily alters (1) the value of a consequence and (2) the likelihood of behavior that has produced that consequence in the past. In the workplace, MOs aren't always as obvious as thirst or hunger, but they're just as real.

Let's say an employee is working toward a promotion. That goal increases the *value* of certain consequences—like recognition, praise, or successful project completion—because those outcomes are now more directly tied to advancement. As a result, behaviors that have historically led to those outcomes (e.g., meeting deadlines, collaborating, problem-solving) are more likely to occur. The same goes for someone who's trying to earn respect from their peers or simply wants to make a meaningful contribution—those motivations change what "counts" as reinforcing in the moment and shift behavior accordingly.

This full sequence is what behavior scientists call the **four-term contingency**: Motivating Operations → Antecedents → Behavior → Consequences. Or simply: **MO → A → B → C**.

What $E=mc^2$ is to physics, **MO→A→B→C** is to behavior. It's the governing formula. Each element plays a role: MO's and antecedents might get behavior going, but it's the **consequences** that carry the heaviest weight. They tell the performer whether the behavior was worth it—whether it should continue or disappear.

Now let's unpack this further using human behavior to show how immediate and long-term contingencies function as proximate and ultimate causes of action. In behavior science, a **contingency** simply refers to the relationship between behavior and its consequences—an **if–then** pattern. *If* I study hard, *then* I pass the test. *If* I show up early, *then* I'm trusted with more responsibility. Over time, these contingencies shape and sustain what we do. Remember the four-term contingency? It's really just a structured series of if–then relationships: if the right motivation is in place, and the right antecedent appears, then behavior occurs—and if it contacts a reinforcing consequence, it's likely to happen again. **Reinforcement** simply means something happens after a behavior that makes it more likely to happen in the future. It's not about praise or prizes—it's about the impact on behavior.

Take the example of a student going to school. On the surface, it's a simple daily routine. But under the hood, it's a complex behavior shaped and maintained by reinforcement occurring across time—**a series of contingencies**, each one connecting behavior to a meaningful outcome:

- **Milliseconds:** The buzz of the alarm triggers a surge of adrenaline—an immediate jolt that begins the momentum.

- **Seconds:** They check their phone and see a motivational message or text from a friend—social connection reinforces engagement.

- **Minutes:** They enjoy the taste of breakfast and the smell of fresh roasted coffee—sensory reinforcement makes the routine pleasant.

- **Hours:** They look forward to a favorite class or seeing a friend at lunch—anticipation keeps behavior moving.

- **Days:** They get positive feedback from a teacher or score well on an assignment—daily reinforcement for effort and skill.

- **Weeks:** They notice progress in a subject that once felt impossible—evidence that their effort is paying off.

- **Months:** They begin building confidence, academic fluency, and a sense of social belonging—contingencies now start aligning with **competence and community**.

- **Years:** They get closer to graduating, accessing future opportunities, and fulfilling personal and family expectations—behavior now connects to **autonomy, achievement, contribution, legacy,** and **lifestyle.**

Each of these layers represents a contingency—an if–then relationship that connects effort to outcome. If I get up and engage, then I contact something valuable. Some of these consequences are proximate or immediate contingencies—a smile, a win, a high grade. Others are ultimate or long-term contingencies—a life of choice, respect, and purpose.

If we look through the lens of behavior science, we can see the full **four-term contingency** at work. The student wakes up with a purpose—perhaps driven by the desire to succeed, gain independence, or make their family proud (**motivating operation**). The sound of the alarm and their schedule act as cues (**antecedents**). They choose to get ready and attend class (**behavior**). Along the way, they receive meaningful outcomes—praise, progress, connection, accomplishment (**consequences**). Every link in that chain plays a role—but it's the **consequences** that ultimately decide whether the behavior continues.

Meaningful behavior is built through a combination of **short-term** and **long-term contingencies**. Immediate consequences—like praise, progress, or relief—create short-term reinforcement that drives momentum. These are the moments when the brain quickly learns, *"If I do this, that will happen."* Finish the report, get a thank-you. Show up on time, avoid correction. That's how behavior gets traction. But over time, as those same behaviors continue to produce outcomes that align with deeper values or long-term goals, **extended contingencies** start to shape direction. Now the pattern becomes, *"If I keep doing this, it moves me closer to who I want to become."* When short- and long-term contingencies are both in play, behavior isn't just repeated—it's anchored in purpose.

Just like species go extinct when their environment stops supporting them, behavior dies out when it no longer produces reinforcing consequences. Take the saber-toothed tiger. Once a dominant predator, it was built for ambush—short bursts of power, massive canine teeth, and prey that moved slowly enough or predictably enough to be caught with that strategy. But then the environment changed. Large herbivores disappeared. Climate shifts altered the landscape. The saber-tooth's behavior—once reinforced by successful hunts—no longer paid off. Over time, the behavior didn't adapt. The species vanished.

That's extinction. Not just biological—*behavioral.*

The same pattern plays out across species. Consider the cheetah. When sprint after sprint ends in failure—no prey caught, no calories gained—it doesn't keep running just because it's "wired" to. It adjusts. Slows down. Conserves energy. Why? Because behavior that isn't reinforced fades. That's environmental feedback in action. Not verbal. Not social. *Functional.*

Now zoom in on human behavior.

Take a student who starts the year strong—completing assignments, participating, staying late to study. But if their effort is consistently met with silence—no recognition, no feedback, no tangible reinforcement—extinction sets in. The behavior that once served a purpose now hits a dead end.

But here's where it gets worse.

If the student's effort is not just ignored but *punished*—mocked by peers, met with more demands, or criticized for "trying too hard"—now we're talking about a different process. **Punishment** occurs when a consequence follows a behavior and makes it *less likely to occur again*. It doesn't require yelling or discipline—it could be subtle. A sarcastic comment. An eye roll. An increased workload. When effort leads to discomfort, we don't just lose momentum. We train avoidance.

So now we've got a double hit:

- **Extinction:** No reinforcement, behavior fades.
- **Punishment:** Aversive consequence, behavior is actively suppressed.

Here's the real cost: when feedback loops break—when effort is either ignored or punished—people don't always leave. Their behavior, on the other hand, does. Sure, they may still show up. But what they do while they're there changes. Initiative vanishes. Creativity dries up. Engagement evaporates.

No reinforcement. No support. No behavior.

Just like species, behavior goes extinct when the environment stops sustaining it.

YOU ARE THE ENVIRONMENT

This brings us to your role as a leader. In nature, species adapt to their environments. But in leadership, you have a unique power: **you are the arranger of the environment**. Your behavior—especially your feedback—is often a crucial part of the environment for others.

Where species can't control their evolutionary environment, *you* can design the conditions that increase the odds of high-performing behavior taking root. The higher you sit on the organizational chart, the greater your opportunity to shape the contingencies and culture that select for excellence.

Let's clarify what we mean by "design the environment." This includes arranging the physical setting, scheduling routines, selecting reinforcement systems, and most importantly, adjusting your own behavior as a leader. What you must understand is that you are not just in the environment. You are often a major part of the environment of others, especially when you are ultimately responsible for their performance. One small tweak in how or when you give feedback can trigger a major shift in someone's behavior.

But even at the team level, you wield influence. You don't have to restructure the whole system. One piece of actionable feedback, one small environmental tweak, can shape behavior toward outcomes that matter. And yes—sometimes that means *you* need to adapt first. Because just like species evolve to fit their context, effective leaders shift their own behavior to produce the conditions where others thrive.

FEEDBACK IS A NECESSITY

Let's go a step further: performance is behavior that produces results—within a specific set of conditions. Consistent performance requires more than good intentions or raw effort. It calls for intentional systems that shape and support the right behavior at the right time. Feedback plays a central role in that process. It directs attention, reinforces progress, and helps fine-tune actions toward meaningful outcomes. In effective leadership, feedback is a core practice—embedded, deliberate, and ongoing.

Leadership is behavior. Culture is behavior. Performance is behavior. Feedback isn't a side task—it's how *you*, as a leader, shape, sustain, and scale all of it.

That's the behavioral challenge.

In an age of performance reviews, engagement surveys, and coaching models, feedback is everywhere—but its impact is inconsistent. That's because many leaders are using tools without understanding the mechanics behind them. And without those mechanics—without the science—feedback becomes a gamble instead of a guarantee.

WHY THIS BOOK IS DIFFERENT

This book is not about buzzwords. It's about what actually works—how feedback functions, how it drives performance, and how leaders can shape, sustain, and scale behavior through deliberate, evidence-based action.

After years of helping leaders—from CEOs and Superintendents to classroom leaders and combat coaches—I've seen firsthand what happens when feedback is intentional… and when it's not. I remember coaching a director who struggled to give timely feedback to their team. Morale was low, and small issues snowballed into bigger ones simply because no one felt seen or guided. Once we implemented a simple system of regular check-ins and behavior-specific praise, things shifted—engagement climbed, and problems were addressed early. It was a clear example of how the presence—or absence—of feedback shapes everything. Whether on the mat or in the boardroom, it's always the same: when feedback flows, performance grows. I've watched teams unlock their potential not because of charisma or cleverness, but because their leaders understood how to deliver meaningful feedback that actually changed behavior.

HOW THIS BOOK WORKS

We'll use the following format for each chapter to get a compre-hensive behavioral understanding of the nuances of effective feedback:

- **The behavioral challenge**
- **The behavioral indicators**
- **The behavioral science behind the behavior**
- **The behavioral solution**

This structure ensures each chapter is both practical and grounded. It starts with defining a common leadership issue, then moves through clear signs to recognize it, the science that explains it, and finally, actionable steps to address it.

Each principle will come alive through real and hypothetical examples, personal insights, and behavior science-backed tools that help you shape performance in real time.

If you want to lead with intention—and create environments where performance, trust, and growth thrive—it starts with feedback.

SUMMARY

Even your best people lose their way when the signals go silent. Feedback provides the direction they need to stay on course. Before we move forward, here's a quick recap:

- Behavior is the engine of all organizational results.
- Just like traits in species are selected over time based on their contribution to survival and reproduction, behaviors in humans are selected by consequences.
- Your feedback is part of the environment that selects behavior. As a leader, you play an active role in shaping that environment—through what you reinforce, what you model, and what you tolerate.

With that clarity, we're ready to dive into the lifeblood of leadership. In the forthcoming chapters, you'll explore the effect feedback has on behavior—the difference between its intended impact and unintended consequences. You'll learn how to harness feedback's power to produce the results you want and lead smarter, not harder, using the science of human behavior.

CHAPTER 1

FEEDBACK ISN'T OPTIONAL— IT'S OXYGEN

WHY FEEDBACK IS ESSENTIAL TO SURVIVAL AND PERFORMANCE, NOT JUST AN HR CHECKBOX

Imagine being in a high-stakes boxing match. You're in the ring, adrenaline pumping, swinging with all you've got. But your coach? Silent. No shouts of encouragement. No strategic corrections. No "keep your left up!" Just silence. How long do you last in that fight?

Feedback is like oxygen in high-pressure moments—it keeps people grounded, responsive, and able to adapt. Without it, performance doesn't just stagnate—it starts to weaken. In leadership, withholding feedback is like cutting off airflow when it's needed most. If you want people to thrive under pressure, you have to keep that oxygen flowing.

Now shift that ring to the workplace. When leaders go quiet, the result isn't bruises—it's **behavioral drift**. That's what happens when performance slowly shifts off course due to a lack of consistent feedback and reinforcement. People stop contacting consequences that clarify what's working and what's not. They start guessing what matters, filling in the gaps with assumptions, or worse—stop caring altogether. That's the real fight leaders face: the behavioral challenge of silence.

What's the Behavioral Challenge?

Too often, leaders treat feedback as an optional add-on— something to schedule, delay, or avoid entirely. But when feed-back is missing, behavior drifts. Performance plateaus. Culture stagnates.

When feedback is inconsistent or nonexistent, confusion spreads. High performers don't know if they're hitting the mark. Struggling team members don't know how to course correct. Over time, this feedback void becomes cultural—people stop expecting recognition and stop expecting change.

This creates a leadership vacuum—one in which misbehavior is tolerated, good behavior goes unrecognized, and underper-formance festers until it turns into resentment or turnover.

The Behavioral Indicators

When feedback fails, the signals show up in the behaviors of both leaders and those they lead. And if you know what to look for, the signs are unmistakable. When feedback fails, you don't need guesswork—you need to observe. The signs live in behavior, both in how leaders respond and how performers react. These indicators reveal the health of your feedback system.

To identify when feedback is faltering, we need to focus on observable behavior—both in ourselves as leaders and in the people we support. The behavioral indicators listed below provide insight into how your system is operating. They can help you detect whether behavior is being reinforced, punished, or ignored—and whether the current contingencies are shaping the performance you're aiming for.

Leader Behavior:

- Avoids giving feedback unless there's a problem
  Example: A manager checks in only when something's wrong but says nothing when goals are met or exceeded.

- Misses opportunities to reinforce effective behavior

  Example: A team member de-escalates a tense customer interaction, and the leader stays silent—no acknowledgment, no follow-up.

- Disengages during key performance moments

  Example: During a team presentation, the leader scrolls through emails instead of being present and offering feedback afterward.

- Responds inconsistently or unpredictably

  Example: One week, a missed deadline is ignored; the next, a minor delay leads to public reprimand—with no clear expectations in place.

- Gives vague "keep it up" feedback without anchoring it in observable behavior

  Example: After a strong performance review, the only comment is, "Just keep doing what you're doing," leaving the performer unclear on what actually worked.

Performer Behavior:

- Operates without clarity on expectations or progress

  Example: A new employee tries different approaches to complete tasks but isn't sure which ones are effective because feedback is missing.

- Guesses at what matters instead of aligning with priorities

  Example: A team member spends hours perfecting a report layout, assuming it's important—only to learn the leader never reads it.

- Becomes hesitant or risk-averse due to lack of direction

  Example: A usually proactive employee stops making decisions independently after being met with silence on past efforts.

- Seeks excessive reassurance to compensate for feedback gaps

  Example: A team member constantly checks in—"Is this what you wanted?"—due to uncertainty about how their performance is being received.

- Disengages or checks out

  Example: A performer who once took initiative now sticks strictly to minimum responsibilities after months of silence from leadership.

These behaviors feed into each other. When leaders don't reinforce behavior that moves the team forward, performers operate in the dark. Without feedback, small problems quietly erode potential—or eventually explode into full-blown performance breakdowns.

Think of a new hire who asks fewer questions over time—not because they're more confident, but because they're not getting answers that help. When performers can't connect effort to outcome, disengagement follows.

The Behavioral Science Behind the Behavior

Feedback is often misunderstood or avoided. It's perceived as confrontational, uncomfortable, or unnecessary—something you give only when something goes wrong.

But in behavior science, feedback is simply a stimulus that changes future behavior. It can be intentional or environmental, vocal or visual, subtle or direct.

Let's be clear: we don't reinforce *people*. We reinforce *behavior*.

And the behavior of delivering feedback—*especially corrective feedback*—is rarely reinforced. In fact, it's often punished. If a leader gives constructive feedback and gets eye-rolling, avoidance, or tension in return, that behavior is less likely to happen again.

Over time, leaders do what all humans do when behavior contacts aversive consequences: they avoid the situation. And silence becomes the default.

Meanwhile, performers are always experiencing consequences— whether leaders are delivering them intentionally or not.

- No response to extra effort? That behavior may fade out.
- A vague nod to a confused directive? That ambiguity might get reinforced.
- Avoiding a challenging task but escaping consequences? That *loafing* might be reinforced through the ease of doing nothing.

The environment is always giving feedback—even if you're not.

SO WHAT DOES FEEDBACK DO, BEHAVIORALLY SPEAKING?

Let's ground this in evolutionary and behavior science. Just like species evolve based on which traits improve survival and reproduction, human behavior is selected by consequences. Organisms allocate behavior in milliseconds, minutes, hours, and days based on what pays off. If the consequence is positive— or removes discomfort—the behavior continues. If it's aversive, it fades.

And feedback? It plays multiple roles in this selection process. Depending on the conditions, it can do one or more of the following (Mangiapanello & Hemmes, 2015):

1. **Start New Behavior**

   Feedback can serve as a cue (or discriminative stimulus, more on this in Chapter 2), signaling that certain behaviors are required or will contact reinforcement. This helps performers engage with new tasks, shift directions, or respond to new expectations.

   Example: "Starting tomorrow, I'd like you to lead the morning huddle—use the checklist as your guide."

2. **Stop Undesired Behavior**

   When feedback highlights errors or calls out counterproductive behavior, it can function as punishment—reducing the likelihood that behavior will happen again. That doesn't mean it has to be harsh. But it does mean it has to be deliberate.

   Example: "When you interrupt during meetings, it shuts others down. Let's wait until people finish before adding your thoughts."

3. **Keep Desired Behavior Going**

   When feedback is specific, timely, and contingent on performance, it serves as positive reinforcement. It strengthens and maintains behavior. This is how you sustain momentum.

   Example: "Your report was clear and concise—that's exactly what we needed. Keep that format."

4. **Motivate Future Behavior**

   Sometimes feedback alters the value of a reinforcer. Think about when someone says, "You're close to hitting your goal." That feedback doesn't reinforce the behavior directly—it increases the motivation to keep going. In behavior science, that's a motivating operation.

Example: "You're just two projects away from qualifying for the bonus tier."

5. **Change or Shape Behavior**

Effective feedback doesn't just reinforce or correct—it shapes. It helps someone move from "almost right" to "that's it." By reinforcing successive approximations or offering precise redirection, feedback gradually molds performance.

Example: "Nice work. Now try pausing before you deliver the final point to give it more impact."

6. **Generate New Behavior Over Time**

Beyond starting or shaping one behavior, feedback can help build behavioral flexibility—broadening a performer's repertoire. Over time, this creates more adaptive, creative, and value-aligned actions that weren't previously part of the person's skillset.

Example: "You've started asking questions that help the team think critically—that's leadership-level behavior."

In short, feedback is a behavioral tool with range. It's not just about praise or correction. It's about *guiding the evolution of behavior* in a way that's intentional, effective, and aligned with meaningful outcomes.

The more leaders understand these functions—and learn to deliver feedback with fluency—the more they'll shape behavior that sustains performance, builds competence, and drives growth.

The Behavioral Solution

When it comes to performance, feedback should function as intentional behavior that shapes other behavior. Every word, gesture, or cue from a leader creates conditions that guide performance—either strengthening fluency or contributing to ambiguity.

Effective leaders don't wait for annual reviews or hope people "figure it out." They actively shape behavior in the moment—on the floor, in meetings, during hallway conversations. And they don't rely on a single method. They use vocal, visual, gestural, and natural feedback delivered through environmental outcomes that help performers connect their actions to meaningful consequences.

A department lead passes by an employee who just wrapped up a tough client call. Without stopping, she says, "That was a tough one—you handled it with patience and professionalism. That builds trust." *That's vocal feedback*: clear, direct, and tied to values.

Later, in a team meeting, a manager nods subtly and raises his eyebrows when a team member shares an idea that aligns with the company's current initiative. Nothing's said, but the performer sees the signal and leans in. *That's visual feedback*: nonverbal reinforcement that still shapes behavior.

In the hallway, a principal walks past a teacher greeting each student at the door. The principal gives a quick thumbs-up as he passes, a simple gesture saying, *"That's the kind of connection we value here." That's gestural feedback*: brief, low-effort, and high-impact.

And then there's natural feedback—the consequence baked into the environment. A nurse double-checks a medication dose and avoids a near-miss. No one has to say a word. The safety of the patient is the feedback. The outcome speaks for itself.

Done right, feedback becomes a fluent part of the culture—real-time, value-driven, and performance-shaping. It's not a task on a to-do list. It's a way of being. And it's how effective leaders make behavior better every day.

DO THIS → NOT THAT

When done right, feedback becomes a fluent part of the culture—real-time, value-driven, and performance-shaping.

Here's how to turn feedback from a vague habit into a powerful leadership behavior:

Do This

Give real-time comments

Example: "That pivot after your jab opened the angle perfectly—do more of that."

Deliver behavior-specific praise

Example: "You stayed focused during the group discussion—your presence helped the team stay on track."

Use multimodal feedback

Example: Give a thumbs-up and a nod immediately after a successful demo, then model the behavior for others.

Leverage natural consequences

Example: "Notice how the customer smiled when you used their name? That connection matters."

Tie feedback to shared values

Example: "Opening the meeting with expectations kept us aligned. That supports our value of clarity."

Not That

Wait for formal reviews to give feedback

Missed opportunities for in-the-moment shaping.

Give general praise like "Good job"

Unclear; doesn't connect the behavior to the result.

Rely only on verbal feedback

Missed chances to model, prompt, or reinforce naturally.

Ignore natural feedback

Overlook powerful, real-time cues that can reinforce behavior.

Give feedback divorced from values

Performer sees no clear "why"—which decreases motivation and makes behavior less likely to maintain over time.

SUMMARY

- ➤ Feedback isn't a formality—it's the heartbeat. Without it, performance flatlines.

- ➤ All behavior is shaped by consequences. If you're not giving feedback, the environment still is.

- ➤ Effective feedback is intentional behavior that changes behavior. Use it deliberately, frequently, and with precision.

- ➤ You don't need to restructure your whole system— sometimes one sentence at the right moment can shape everything.

Remember, when feedback flows, performance grows. But when it doesn't, confusion, disengagement, and inconsistency take its place. Even high performers can get lost when the signals go silent.

In the next chapter, we explore how feedback loops break down—and what to do when your team stops listening.

CHAPTER 2

VAGUE PRAISE, VAGUE RESULTS

WHEN ENCOURAGEMENT DOESN'T TRANSLATE INTO ACTION

Imagine being told "great job" after a big presentation. You smile, say thanks, and walk away. But what *exactly* was great? The data analysis? The clarity of the message? The calm delivery? Or just the fact that you didn't bomb it?

This kind of ambiguous praise might feel good in the moment, but it's useless for improving performance. Praise like that doesn't tell you what to repeat—or what to adjust. It's noise masquerading as a signal. If Chapter 1 showed us that feedback is oxygen—essential for survival—this chapter tackles the next problem: feedback that keeps people breathing but doesn't help them grow. Vague feedback is like air without direction—it keeps them alive but doesn't move them forward.

Vague praise. Broad correction. General encouragement. These all suffer from the same flaw—they lack behavioral specificity. Without identifying the precise actions that led to success or failure, feedback becomes mere commentary rather than a tool for shaping future behavior.

What's the Behavioral Challenge?

Many leaders understand that positive feedback is important. While they're not wrong, simply being positive isn't enough. Feedback needs to be precise and timely to actually influence behavior (Alvero et al., 2001). Praise like "good job" or "you're killing it" may feel reinforcing in the moment, but without clarity, it leaves people guessing.

It gets worse when correction is vague too. Saying things like "That wasn't great" or "Let's do better next time" gives no direction. These statements might even trigger anxiety or resentment, because people don't know what they did wrong or how to improve. That's not feedback—it's a drive-by. Quick, vague, and gone before the performer knows what actually hit them.

Here's the deeper behavioral challenge: leaders often believe they've provided feedback when they've just spoken in generalities. It creates a feedback mirage: the feeling of input when there's really none there. If performers act on that mirage, they can instead drift further from desired performance rather than closer to it.

So, what's the result? Confusion, frustration, and a lack of behavior change. People either keep doing what they're doing or disengage altogether; meanwhile, the leader is left wondering why things aren't improving.

The Behavioral Indicators

We can't change what we don't observe. So, what should we look for when we suspect that vague feedback is a problem? These indicators provide insight into how both the leader and performer are behaving—and where the feedback loop is breaking down. It's important to note that performer behavior is often a reflection of leadership performance.

Leader Behavior:

- Uses general praise like "Good job" without naming the behavior

Example: A team member saves a project from going off-track and the leader says, "Nice save!"—but doesn't say what was done or how it helped.

- Says things like "Let's just do better next time" without direction

  Example: After a missed deadline, the leader addresses the whole team with "We have to tighten things up," offering no specifics about what needs to change.

- Gives performance reviews full of buzzwords but light on detail

  Example: An employee's annual review says they "demonstrate leadership potential," but no examples are given, and no next steps are laid out.

- Delivers correction with phrases like "You need to step up" or "This isn't your best work" without explaining which aspects missed the mark

  Example: After a client call that didn't go well, a supervisor says, "That wasn't great," but doesn't explain what should've gone differently.

- Reinforces effort without addressing impact

  Example: "Thanks for staying late," with no mention of whether the extra time actually improved the outcome.

Performer Behavior:

- Repeats ineffective behavior, unsure what to change

  Example: A sales rep keeps using the same script that isn't converting—because no one told them why it isn't working.

- Stops innovating or trying new approaches due to lack of clarity

  Example: A creative team member stops pitching bold ideas after getting only vague "thanks" instead of detailed feedback.

- Becomes overly reliant on reassurance and validation

  Example: An employee constantly asks, "Was that okay?" after routine tasks because past feedback lacked clarity and direction.

- Asks fewer clarifying questions and avoids feedback

  Example: A performer begins to disengage and avoid feedback sessions altogether, assuming they'll just be vague or unhelpful.

- Becomes frustrated or disengaged when correction feels arbitrary

  Example: A team member is reprimanded in front of others with "This isn't how we do things," but they were never told how things should be done.

The Behavioral Science Behind the Behavior

There's no discriminative stimulus to signal what's working—or what's not. In behavior science, a **discriminative stimulus** (or **SD**) is a cue in the environment that signals when a certain behavior is likely to be reinforced. In everyday life, that could be a green light telling us it's safe to go—because we've learned that going at a green light helps us get to our destination efficiently, while stopping at a red light helps us avoid tickets or accidents. Or it might be the sound of a microwave dinging, signaling that food is ready and reinforcing our cooking with a warm meal. These cues shape our behavior because they're consistently tied to reinforcing consequences.

In the workplace, when those cues are missing—when no one signals what behavior is effective or expected—people are left guessing. And guessing is no way to build consistent performance.

This is where feedback breaks down. In behavioral terms, vague praise is a weak reinforcer—it doesn't clearly tell someone what they did right, so it doesn't increase the chances they'll do it again. And vague correction? It's not helpful—it's just criticism without direction. It can make people feel bad or defensive, but it doesn't show them how to improve. That's how fear-based cultures form: not from loud yelling, but from a steady drip of negative, nonspecific feedback that leaves people walking on eggshells and unsure of where they stand.

Vague feedback also creates something called **response generalization**—that's when a person tries a bunch of different behaviors hoping one of them is "the right one," because they have no idea what triggered the praise or correction. **In everyday terms, it's like throwing darts in the dark.** You keep guessing, adjusting, overcompensating—until eventually, you burn out or give up. That scattershot effort doesn't build precision or progress—it builds frustration.

And here's the trap: leaders rarely receive feedback on their feedback effectiveness. Which means they keep delivering vague comments, thinking they're helping. But they're actually creating a fog that clouds performance.

The Behavioral Solution

Too often, feedback becomes background noise—well-intentioned but ineffective. Generic praise like "Great job" or vague correction like "Be more careful" doesn't tell the performer what to do more of—or how to improve. Why? Because it lacks the four features essential for influencing behavior:

- Specificity means naming the exact behavior. Instead of "Nice work," say, "I appreciated how you clarified the customer's concern before offering a solution." Specific feedback tells the performer *what* worked.

- Timing is about delivering feedback as close to the behavior as possible. The longer you wait, the weaker the connection. Immediate feedback strengthens the link between action and outcome.

- Purpose ties the behavior to a bigger value or goal. It answers the question: *Why does this behavior matter?* For example: "That follow-up call shows we're committed to client satisfaction."

- Actionability means the feedback leads to a clear next step—either reinforcing what to keep doing or guiding what to change. "Be more careful" doesn't cut it. "Double-check the dosage before signing off" does.

When feedback is specific, timely, purposeful, and actionable, it functions as an effective tool for shaping behavior. It creates clarity, reinforces desired actions, and helps performers move in the right direction.

DO THIS → NOT THAT

To be useful, feedback must act like a GPS, not a billboard. It should give clear direction, reinforce desired movement, and help the performer navigate. Whether reinforcing or correcting, your feedback should answer the performer's unspoken question: *What exactly should I keep doing, stop doing, or do differently—and why?*

Let's look at how to move from vague noise to actionable signal:

Do This

"You asked a great follow-up question during that meeting. It showed the client we were listening and helped clarify their needs."
Reinforces a specific, value-adding behavior.

"When you used the visual timeline in the proposal, it made the steps really easy to follow. Let's make that a standard going forward."

Highlights a concrete example and promotes generalization.

"I noticed you jumped in to help when the call queue got backed up—that teamwork kept us on track for response time. That's the kind of support we need more of."

Links effort to a meaningful, observable impact.

"I saw that the weekly report was submitted without the client notes. Those notes drive our strategy conversations, so we need those in every time."

Describes the gap, explains why it matters, and sets a clear expectation.

"In the presentation, the data slides lacked context. Next time, let's pair each chart with a takeaway so it's clear why it matters."

Provides direction and a simple model for improvement.

Not That

"Nice job today."

No idea what behavior was effective—it's vague and non-actionable.

"We need more visuals."

Too broad—leaves the performer guessing what you want.

"Thanks for helping out."

Non-contingent, easily forgotten praise without context.

"Don't forget the details."

Vague, punitive tone with no behavior-specific guidance.

"Make this clearer."

Lacks actionable detail—leaves the performer uncertain about what to fix.

SUMMARY

Vague feedback is a behavioral dead end. It creates ambiguity, undermines motivation, and stalls growth. Leaders may feel like they're reinforcing or correcting, but if their words don't specify behavior, they aren't shaping anything. And if they aren't shaping behavior, they aren't leading.

Let's bring it home:

> The best leaders don't just speak—they signal.

> Praise that lacks specificity doesn't reinforce—it flatters and fades.

> Correction without clarity frustrates rather than fixes.

> Behavior doesn't change when feedback is cloudy—it changes when it's clear.

So ,ask yourself: Are your words helping your team see what success looks like—or are they throwing darts in the dark, hoping something hits the mark?

The difference between feedback that *feels good* and feedback that *does good* is precision. And that's where leadership lives.

CHAPTER 3

THE ECHO EFFECT—WHAT YOU REINFORCE REPEATS

UNDERSTANDING HOW PATTERNS OF REINFORCEMENT SHAPE CULTURE AND HABITS

Picture a department where people show up on time, collaborate effectively, and speak up with new ideas. Those behaviors reflect a system where reinforcement has consistently shaped and supported what the organization values. In other settings, different patterns emerge—employees might coast, avoid risk, or do the bare minimum. These outcomes are also shaped by the contingencies in place. Culture forms through repeated interactions with consequences, whether designed intentionally or not.

In every environment, behavior produces consequences. And those consequences either strengthen or weaken the likelihood that behavior will happen again. That's the echo effect: behavior doesn't just occur once and disappear. It repeats and strengthens when it contacts reinforcement. It fades when it doesn't. Over time, patterns of reinforcement create performance norms—and those norms become culture.

Whether you're aware of it or not, you are reinforcing behavior every day. And if you're not shaping it deliberately, you're still shaping it—just probably not in the direction you want.

What's the Behavioral Challenge?

Leaders often unintentionally reinforce the wrong behavior—or fail to reinforce the right one. They reward compliance over creativity. They give attention to the loudest complainers instead of the quiet contributors. They respond with urgency to crises but ignore consistent, value-adding performance. For example, a manager might drop everything to deal with an employee who constantly misses deadlines and causes disruptions—while never acknowledging the team member who quietly delivers high-quality work ahead of schedule. Over time, that quiet high performer starts to wonder, *"What's the point?"* And then leaders wonder why dysfunctions become the norm.

The problem isn't just what leaders reinforce—it's also what they overlook. Inconsistent reinforcement creates confusion.

It sends the message that doing more or doing better doesn't matter. And when high-effort behavior and low-effort behavior are met with the same consequence—or no consequence at all—people do what behavior science predicts: they conserve energy. That's called response effort—the more energy a behavior requires, the more it needs to be reinforced to be sustained. Without reinforcement, people stop investing effort. In short, they stop trying.

A team member stays late to prep for a big presentation, double-checks the data, and delivers a clear, compelling message. That's high-effort behavior: time investment, attention to detail, and thoughtful delivery. But they receive the same generic "Thanks" as someone who threw together slides at the last minute and winged it during the meeting. That's low-effort behavior: minimal prep, surface-level work, and rushed execution.

Over time, the high-effort behaviors fade because they aren't being meaningfully reinforced. Meanwhile, the low-effort behaviors continue—because they contact the same consequence. The system isn't deliberately rewarding poor performance, but by failing to differentiate, it shapes a pattern such that doing less becomes just as effective as doing more.

This chapter confronts the core issue: most leaders reinforce accidentally rather than strategically. They reinforce what's easy to see, what's loud, or what's urgent, but they fail to reinforce what drives long-term value: daily behaviors that build long term results. That's how mediocrity becomes the standard.

The Behavioral Indicators

Before you can change what you reinforce, you have to recognize the patterns. Here are some signs that reinforcement isn't shaping behavior the way it should—broken down by both leader and performer behavior.

Leader Behavior:

- Publicly praises outcomes without acknowledging the process or effort

  Example: A manager congratulates a team for hitting their monthly goal but fails to recognize the staff member who worked nights to close the final deal. The team hears applause, but the high-effort behavior behind it goes unnoticed.

- Spends more time addressing mistakes than celebrating improvement

  Example: A supervisor emails a staff member every time a report is late but says nothing after three consecutive on-time submissions. The performer starts to feel that progress doesn't matter—only mistakes do.

- Ignores consistent, dependable performers while over-focusing on "problem" staff

  Example: A team member who always shows up early, helps others, and meets goals gets little attention. Meanwhile, the leader holds daily check-ins with the underperformer. The quiet achiever starts to question whether dependability is even valued.

- Delivers reinforcement randomly, without linking it clearly to behavior

  Example: A leader occasionally gives out gift cards or says, "Great job today" with no context. Staff smile, say thanks, but have no clue what behavior led to the praise—so they can't replicate it.

Performer Behavior:

- Focuses on avoiding errors instead of pursuing excellence

  Example: A team member double-checks every tiny detail, afraid of being called out, but avoids taking initiative or making suggestions. They're more focused on not messing up than on contributing meaningfully.

- Reluctant to take initiative after previous efforts went unnoticed

  Example: After once proposing a successful workflow change with no acknowledgment, an employee sticks to the basics. They do what's expected and nothing more—because last time, the extra effort led nowhere.

- Becomes disengaged or performs to the bare minimum

  Example: A reliable employee used to take on new projects eagerly. Now they clock in, do what's required, and clock out—because nothing about going the extra mile ever seemed to matter.

- Looks for shortcuts or ways to "game" reinforcement

  Example: A staff member notices that last-minute heroics get more attention than steady performance—so they start delaying work to create urgency. It's not good for the team, but it gets noticed.

Think of a team member who consistently meets deadlines with high-quality work. If that behavior is never acknowledged, the performer may assume it's expected and unrewarded. Over time, they may begin to slow down, cut corners, or disengage entirely. Not because they stopped caring—but because the environment stopped reinforcing.

Meanwhile, another team member who always runs into last-minute crises gets a surge of support and attention from leadership. Their behavior is inadvertently reinforced—rewarding chaos and neglecting consistency.

Without clear reinforcement strategies, culture is built reactively instead of intentionally. And culture, behaviorally speaking, is just the pattern of shared behaviors shaped by the consequences in that environment. When reinforcement is inconsistent or absent, those patterns develop by accident—not design. That's how leaders end up with teams that do "just enough" rather than consistently striving toward excellence.

It took evolution 3.7 billion years for the environment to shape modern *Homo sapiens*—but you can help create an environment

THE FEEDBACK EFFECT | Dr. Paul Gavoni

that shapes a high-functioning team in three months or less. (Or your money back!)

The Behavioral Science Behind the Behavior

At the heart of behavior science is a simple truth: behavior that is reinforced is more likely to occur again. Reinforcement doesn't mean praise or prizes. It means any consequence that follows a behavior and increases the likelihood of that behavior happening again—whether that consequence is social, environmental, or task-related.

In applied settings, this often happens accidentally. A manager may thank an employee for working late but never reinforce proactive time management—like planning ahead, prioritizing tasks, or asking for support early to avoid last-minute scrambles. A supervisor may unintentionally reinforce complaining by giving complainers extra attention or leniency. These patterns shape future behavior. Over time, putting out fires gets rewarded, and prevention gets ignored.

Reinforcement also explains the power of culture. When teams begin to recognize what gets reinforced—what earns attention, approval, or results—they start replicating those behaviors.

Over time, this becomes the behavioral blueprint of the group. Even subtle cues can shape those group norms. A nod in a meeting. A raised eyebrow. A quick Slack message. While they may appear to be everyday interactions, they operate as feedback events that carry real consequences—shaping which behaviors grow and which fade.

Whether it's vocal ("Nice job handling that"), visual (a thumbs-up emoji), gestural (a smile or head shake), or natural (a smoother workflow or positive outcome), every form of feedback influences behavior. When those signals are consistent and aligned with what the organization values, culture forms by design—not by accident.

The problem isn't that leaders don't care. It's that most haven't been taught to observe, label, and reinforce behavior deliberately. That's where behavioral fluency comes in. Not just knowing *what* to reinforce, *when* to reinforce it, and *why* it matters—but being able to do it smoothly, accurately, and on the fly, even under pressure.

Fluency is the byproduct of well-designed training. It's what turns theory into real-time leadership behavior resulting in automatic and precise responses. In short—good habits.

The Behavioral Solution

Recognition is nice—but reinforcement is how you shape a culture. It's not about making people feel good; it's about making the right behaviors more likely. And that takes intention. Too often, leaders default to outcome-based praise, missing the daily behaviors that drive success. Without timely, behavior-specific reinforcement, people are left guessing at what "good" really means. Worse, they may stop engaging in the very behaviors you want more of. Effective reinforcement targets the process, not just the product—it strengthens what's working so it continues, grows, and spreads. Below are common reinforcement missteps—and what to do instead to ensure your culture thrives on behavior that matters.

DO THIS → NOT THAT

Here are a few examples to guide your reinforcement strategy:

Do This

Reinforce effort and strategy.

Example: "You clearly mapped out each phase before launching the campaign. That preparation helped us avoid delays."

Reinforce behavior immediately when it happens.

Example: Right after a meeting, pull someone aside and say, "Your summary at the end helped the group stay focused. That's leadership."

Acknowledge consistency and reliability.

Example: "You're always the first to update your metrics dashboard. That kind of consistency keeps our reporting strong."

Align reinforcement with values and long-term goals.

Example: "Thanks for flagging that ethical concern early. That protects our credibility with clients."

Not That

Praise only the result.

Example: "Nice job on the campaign numbers." (Leaves out the behavior that produced them.)

Save praise for end-of-year reviews or awards ceremonies.

Example: "You've been doing great all year"—without reinforcing specific behaviors in real time.

Only reinforce when someone 'goes above and beyond.'

Example: Waiting until someone works overtime to say, "Great job," while ignoring the reliable daily effort.

Reinforce shortcuts that achieve results at the expense of process.

Example: "Well, at least we hit the target," even though the method undermined quality or teamwork.

Let's say a team member starts taking more initiative in meetings—bringing new ideas, offering to lead projects. A vague, "Nice work today" won't cut it. But saying, "I noticed you took the lead on that discussion—it moved the conversation forward. Keep doing that," provides specific, timely reinforcement that links the behavior to impact.

Leaders can also ask themselves:

- What behaviors do I want to see more of?
- Am I reinforcing those behaviors when I see them?
- Do my team members know why their behavior matters?

Your answers to these questions will tell you whether your reinforcement strategy is building excellence—or echoing inconsistency.

SUMMARY

Reinforcement is happening all the time, whether you intend it or not. And what you reinforce repeats. That's the echo effect.

To build a culture of excellence, leaders must become fluent in reinforcement—recognizing when behavior happens, delivering reinforcement with clarity and consistency, and aligning that reinforcement with meaningful outcomes.

Here's what to remember:

➤ Culture is built on repeated behavior—and repeated behavior is built on reinforcement.

➤ What you overlook is just as important as what you reward.

➤ Random, vague, or reactive reinforcement builds confusion—not culture.

➤ The most powerful leaders shape performance deliberately, not by accident.

Ask yourself: What am I reinforcing? And is it what I *want* to reinforce?

Your behavior is building something—whether you mean to or not. And what you build becomes the environment your team operates in.

Reinforce deliberately. Because what you reinforce will echo across your culture.

CHAPTER 4

FEEDBACK IS A MIRROR, NOT A MALLET

CULTIVATING SELF-AWARENESS AND DELIVERING FEEDBACK WITHOUT TRIGGERING DEFENSIVENESS

Picture this: a team lead walks into a one-on-one meeting with a tired sigh and says, "Listen, this needs to stop. You keep missing deadlines." The employee tenses. Shoulders rise. Eye contact drops. The conversation derails before it even begins.

In moments like this, it's easy to blame the employee for being too sensitive, too fragile, too defensive. But the uncomfortable truth is that it's not only *what* you say—it's *how* it lands. And often, it lands wrong.

Feedback is one of the most powerful tools in a leader's toolbox. But when misused, it doesn't motivate, it suppresses. It doesn't guide, it wounds. Instead of shaping behavior, feedback becomes an aversive event that people learn to avoid.

That's why the best leaders don't use feedback like a mallet. They use it like a mirror—helping people see what's working, what's not, and how to grow without fear of humiliation or punishment.

What's the Behavioral Challenge?

Leaders often misunderstand the behavioral impact of how feedback is delivered. When feedback becomes associated with negative emotions—embarrassment, fear, shame—it triggers what behavior analysts call an **escape-maintained response**. In plain terms: people will start doing whatever they can to avoid it.

This includes:

- Dodging conversations
- Avoiding eye contact
- Withholding ideas
- Becoming quiet in meetings
- Or worse—leaving the organization entirely

I remember working with a team in which one high-performing employee suddenly went quiet. She stopped offering suggestions, pulled back in meetings, and started avoiding her supervisor.

On paper, she looked like she was still doing her job—but the spark was gone. When I asked her about it privately, she told me, "It's just not worth it. Every time I speak up, I leave feeling smaller. So, I just stopped speaking."

This is what happens when feedback is delivered like a blunt instrument. The behavior being shaped isn't better performance—it's avoidance. And that avoidance often becomes habitual, not situational.

The root cause? A mismatch between the **motivating operation** (MO) and the feedback itself. Remember that in behavior science, an MO is what increases or decreases the value of a consequence at a given time. For example, when someone is already stressed, even mild criticism can feel intense. That person is more motivated to escape than engage. If the leader doesn't consider this, they may deliver feedback in a way that triggers resistance—even if the content is accurate.

This is why timing, tone, and delivery matter as much as the message. If people feel unsafe or attacked, they stop listening and start self-protecting. And once that pattern forms, feedback no longer serves its function—it becomes a trigger.

The Behavioral Indicators

When feedback is used carelessly, it backfires. Instead of shaping better performance, it conditions avoidance. These behavioral indicators reveal whether feedback is functioning as a mirror for growth—or a mallet that people brace for. And remember, behavior always tells the story.

Leader Behavior:

- **Opens with criticism rather than curiosity**
  Example: A manager starts a one-on-one with, "I need to talk to you about everything that went wrong last week," instead of asking, "How did you think that project went?" This signals blame, not collaboration.

- **Focuses on errors without pointing to next steps**
  Example: A department head says, "You completely missed the mark," but offers no guidance on how to improve. The performer leaves unsure of what to change.

- **Delivers feedback in front of others**
  Example: A supervisor says during a team huddle, "You all need to learn how to show up on time—especially you, Jamie." That's not feedback. It's public shaming.

- **Uses sarcasm or a judgmental tone**

  Example: "Oh great, another brilliant idea from the marketing genius," a leader quips during a meeting. It's masked as humor but lands as ridicule.

- **Misses the opportunity for response or dialogue**

  Example: A leader sends an email listing performance issues but doesn't invite a conversation. There's no space to ask questions or clarify expectations—just a unilateral directive.

Performer Behavior:

- **Avoids asking questions or initiating conversations**

  Example: A team member who used to ask clarifying questions now stays silent—even when uncertain—because past questions were met with eye rolls or dismissiveness.

- **Shows visible discomfort during check-ins**

  Example: During one-on-ones, a direct report crosses their arms, gives short answers, and constantly glances at the clock—signaling psychological withdrawal.

- **Offers defensive or minimal responses**

  Example: When given feedback, someone quickly says, "Okay, fine," or "Got it," without making eye contact. It's not acceptance—it's a shield.

- **Stops volunteering ideas or taking risks**

  Example: A staff member who once contributed regularly to brainstorm sessions now says nothing, afraid any misstep will bring criticism.

- **Appears disengaged or checked out**

  Example: You notice a team member avoiding meetings, missing deadlines, or clocking out emotionally. It's not laziness—it's learned helplessness in response to chronic negative feedback.

Together, these behaviors tell a clear story: feedback has become something to endure, not something to learn from. And when feedback feels like a threat, growth halts and psychological safety erodes. That's why shaping your feedback delivery is a critical leadership responsibility.

The Behavioral Science Behind the Behavior

As you've learned, feedback is often considered a consequence—it follows behavior and influences whether that behavior happens again. But feedback can also serve as an antecedent (Mangiapanello & Hemmes, 2015), especially when it signals expectations or prompts behavior moving forward. In fact, feedback often functions as both: a consequence for what just happened and an antecedent for what comes next. Still, it only works if the consequence that follows is reinforcing. If the consequence is punishing—even unintentionally—it can reduce the chances of the behavior happening again.

For example, a team member steps up to lead a meeting for the first time. Afterward, the leader gives detailed "constructive" criticism in front of the group. The intent was for the feedback to guide future performance—to serve as an antecedent. But it functioned as a punisher. The performer walked away feeling embarrassed. The consequence wasn't reinforcing—it was aversive. Next time, they hesitate to step up at all.

This is where **motivating operations (MOs)** matter. If someone is already under pressure, your feedback may not be reinforcing , even if it's well-intentioned. It might instead evoke escape-maintained responses, causing the person to avoid the conversation entirely.

Let's say a team member just received critical comments from a client. You walk in and say, "We need to talk about that presentation." Even if your feedback is balanced and constructive, their current MO is escape—they're already bracing for more bad news. Your words will be filtered through that lens unless you set the stage differently.

It's also important to remember that some people have a learning history such that feedback was consistently aversive—used as a tool for punishment or control. In those cases, even neutral feedback may be met with resistance until a new history of reinforcement is built.

The goal isn't to walk on eggshells. It's to deliver feedback in a way that maximizes the likelihood of behavior change and minimizes emotional retreat. That means shifting feedback from something people fear to something they *seek*.

The Behavioral Solution

Feedback can take many forms, and the way it's delivered shapes how it's received. Sometimes it hits like a mallet—blunt and forceful, leading to avoidance. Other times it functions like a mirror—reflective and clarifying, increasing the likelihood of behavior change. These outcomes are influenced by factors such as trust, timing, and behavioral precision—key elements that determine whether feedback supports growth or disrupts it.

Leaders who want feedback to be heard—and acted on—must shape the conditions under which it's delivered. This means moving beyond corrective conversations and creating a culture in which feedback is consistent, reinforcing part of learning and growth. From a behavior science perspective, feedback only functions when it informs future behavior, not just critiques the past. If your goal is to improve performance, not just point out problems, your feedback should reflect that. Here's how to shift from confrontation to collaboration:

- **Start with safety.** Before feedback is accepted, the person must feel psychologically safe. That means building trust over time—not just during the initial conversation.

- **Ask before you tell.** Questions like "How do you think that went?" promote self-evaluation and open the door for dialogue.

- **Focus on behavior, not traits.** For example: "You interrupted twice in the meeting" instead of "You're being disrespectful."

- **Invite reflection.** "What would you do differently next time?" helps transfer ownership of the solution.

- **Follow up with reinforcement.** When improvements happen, acknowledge them. Reinforcement closes the loop and strengthens future engagement.

Feedback as a Tool for Self-Shaping

When delivered with intention, feedback doesn't just guide— it teaches people how to shape their own behavior. That's the ultimate goal: developing self-aware performers who reflect, adjust, and improve without waiting for external correction.

Over time, high-quality feedback helps people internalize standards. They stop guessing and start assessing their perfomance against what matters. That's when feedback becomes a mirror—not something held up by someone else, but something they carry with them.

In behavior science, fluent habits develop through repeated contact with clear antecedents and meaningful consequences. That's how fluency is built—by arranging conditions where the right cues are followed by reinforcing outcomes. As a result, people respond more accurately, quickly, and confidently—even under pressure.

Leaders play a key role in shaping those conditions—not just through what they say, but how consistently, clearly, and respectfully they say it.

DO THIS → NOT THAT

That's the power of fluent leadership—creating environments where the right cues are followed by reinforcing outcomes. When leaders consistently deliver clear, value-aligned feedback, they help shape not just performance in the moment, but habits that last.

And while the science can get technical, the application doesn't have to be. It comes down to simple, intentional behaviors repeated over time.

Here's how to shape feedback that shapes behavior—instead of shutting it down:

Do This

Ask: "How do you think it went?" before giving input

Example: "Before I share my thoughts, I'm curious—how did that feel for you?"

Highlight the behavior and its impact

Example: "When you paused and clarified the client's concerns, it turned the whole conversation around."

Offer feedback in private

Example: Pulling someone aside after a team huddle to give corrective input in a respectful space.

Link feedback to a shared goal or value

Example: "Helping each other stay on protocol keeps our clients safe—and that's why I'm pointing this out."

Reinforce improvements publicly to model learning culture

Example: "I want to recognize how Sam handled that tough situation—he used the exact strategy we've been training on."

Not That

Lead with: "We need to talk about your mistakes."

Example: Jumping straight into critique without inviting reflection.

Label the person with a judgment

Example: "You're careless." or "You're not cut out for this."

Call someone out in front of peers

Example: "Why would you do that?" said in front of a group.

Base feedback on your own frustration

Example: "This is driving me nuts," instead of tying it to performance goals.

Only comment when things go wrong

Example: Staying silent when performance improves but jumping in when it slips.

SUMMARY

Feedback is one of the most powerful forces in leadership— but only when it's used with care. When delivered poorly, it becomes something people avoid. When delivered well, it becomes something people grow from.

If we want people to take feedback seriously, we must first make it safe. That doesn't mean being soft—it means being precise, respectful, and behavior-specific.

Here's what to remember:

- Feedback shapes behavior, but only if it's not experienced as punishment.

- Motivating operations influence how feedback is received—timing and context matter.

- Defensiveness is a behavioral signal—don't punish it. Understand it.

- Feedback is most effective when it encourages self-reflection, not self-protection.

- The goal is fluency, not fear. And that requires consistency, trust, and reinforcement.

Feedback is a mirror. When people can look into it and see where they're going—not just where they've fallen—you'll build a culture where learning, not hiding, is the norm.

CHAPTER 5

ONE-SIZE FEEDBACK DOESN'T FIT ALL

ADAPTING FEEDBACK TO THE INDIVIDUAL, THE BEHAVIOR, AND THE MOMENT

Imagine two team members on your staff. One thrives on quick, verbal feedback. The other prefers written summaries to reflect on. You've been giving both the same kind of real-time verbal praise—and only one is improving. The other seems to be pulling back. What gives?

Feedback isn't one-size-fits-all. And when we assume it is, we confuse fairness with sameness. Fair doesn't mean identical—it means effective. This chapter explores how tailoring your feedback to individual needs aligns with the core principles of behavior science and supports meaningful performance change.

What's the Behavioral Challenge?

Inconsistent impact. That's the problem. Leaders provide the same type of feedback to everyone, expecting consistent results—but people aren't wired the same way. Different roles, personalities, experience levels, and reinforcement histories all influence how feedback is received, processed, and acted upon.

So, what happens when feedback isn't adapted?

- It becomes noise for some.

- It feels patronizing to others.

- It accidentally reinforces disengagement or creates confusion.

Behaviorally speaking, feedback is only valuable if it functions. If it doesn't change behavior, it's not feedback—it's commentary.

The Behavioral Indicators

When feedback isn't calibrated to the individual, it loses effectiveness and can generate friction. Leaders may believe they're supporting growth, but if the delivery doesn't align with how someone receives and processes feedback, the result is often confusion, withdrawal, or misinterpretation. These behavioral mismatches can disrupt performance and gradually weaken trust and motivation over time.

Below are common observable patterns that signal feedback isn't landing—not because it's wrong, but because it's misdelivered.

Leader Behavior:

- **Uses the same feedback method for every team member regardless of role or personality**

  Example: A manager delivers all feedback via long email write-ups, even for frontline staff who thrive on face-to-face interaction. As a result, those staff members either miss the emails or misinterpret the tone.

- **Overuses public praise or criticism assuming it's always motivating**

  Example: A leader regularly announces "Employee of the Month" without asking if that kind of spotlight matters—or demotivates—some team members. One high performer, uncomfortable with attention, starts pulling back to avoid being singled out.

- **Ignores differences in how team members best process feedback (e.g., auditory vs. visual)**

  Example: During onboarding, a supervisor verbally walks a new hire through feedback on a complex report. The new hire nods along but continues making formatting errors because they process best with visual examples and checklists.

- **Applies performance review templates without room for individual nuance**

  Example: In a review, a team lead uses a generic form that asks everyone to rate their "teamwork" and "initiative," but fails to tailor goals or feedback to the unique responsibilities of specialized roles like developers or creatives.

- **Speaks in broad strokes rather than connecting feedback to individual goals or motivators**

  Example: A director tells a team member, "You're doing a great job—keep it up," without referencing the team member's goal of becoming a lead. The feedback feels flat because it doesn't acknowledge the path they care about.

Performer Behavior:

- **Doesn't act on feedback, even when accurate**

  Example: An employee receives vague praise like "nice work," but has no clue what behavior it referred to—so they keep doing everything the same, including the parts that weren't effective.

- **Seems confused or anxious after receiving input**

  Example: A junior analyst appears visibly flustered during feedback conversations. When asked why, they share that the fast-paced verbal corrections don't give them enough time to process what's expected.

- **Withdraws from future interactions involving performance conversations**

  Example: A designer starts skipping optional check-ins with their team lead after a few feedback sessions felt rushed and overly critical. They say, "I'd rather just get the notes later."

- **Begins to avoid tasks where feedback is likely**

  Example: A team member stops volunteering to lead projects after being publicly critiqued in front of peers.

The feedback wasn't wrong—it was just delivered in a way that triggered embarrassment, not engagement.

- **Responds better to feedback from others (e.g., peers or written formats)**
  Example: A team member struggles to absorb feedback in one-on-one meetings but thrives when peers provide notes through shared documents. It's not resistance—it's a preference for context and time to reflect.

These indicators don't point to a lack of effort or care—they point to misalignment. When we deliver feedback in a format that doesn't resonate, we create unnecessary barriers to growth. The fix isn't to hold back—it's to adapt. Because when the delivery works, so does the feedback.

The Behavioral Science Behind the Behavior

If you recall from earlier, evolutionary science teaches us that traits are selected by the environment—those that lead to survival and reproduction become more common over time. Behavior works the same way. In behavior analysis, we say that consequences select behavior—meaning the environment reinforces certain actions, making them more likely to occur again. But for that selection to happen, the consequence must be meaningful and accessible to the individual. If it's unclear, irrelevant, or delayed, it won't shape behavior—it'll just be noise.

Feedback should function as a discriminative stimulus (SD). Remember, that's a cue signaling that reinforcement is available for a specific behavior. But when the format of the feedback doesn't align with the recipient's learning history, past reinforcement experiences, or current role demands, it may instead function as an S-delta (a signal that reinforcement is not available)—or worse, as a conditioned punisher.

For example:

- A manager gives real-time corrective feedback during a high-stakes task. The intention is for the feedback to serve as an SD—a cue that improvement will contact reinforcement (e.g., recognition, praise, increased trust). But the employee, already under pressure and with a history of being criticized in front of others, experiences it as a signal that no matter how they adjust, reinforcement isn't coming. The feedback now functions as an S-delta—a cue that effort will not be rewarded. If the correction is delivered harshly or publicly, it can even become a conditioned punisher, decreasing the likelihood that the person will take initiative in the future.

- Another example: a visually-oriented performer receives a dense stream of verbal feedback. The leader intends it to be an SD for skill development (i.e., "If you improve this behavior, reinforcement—like more responsibility or growth—will follow"). But because the performer can't process the feedback, it becomes functionally an S-delta—the behavior doesn't lead to reinforcement because the signal wasn't usable. The performer walks away confused, not motivated.

Just think about SDs and S-deltas as reminders that your feedback is always sending a signal—whether you mean to or not. You're either telling people, *"Keep going—this behavior leads to something good,"* or *"Doesn't matter what you do, nothing changes,"* or worse, *"Speak up, and you'll regret it."* The impact depends not just on what you say, but how, when, and to whom you say it.

Behavioral momentum stalls when the feedback loop doesn't connect to the behavior functionally. Feedback that's not "received" in the right form never contacts the behavior it's meant to change.

This is where understanding learning histories and preferences becomes essential. Leaders must become behavior detectives— learning what conditions support feedback functioning as reinforcement.

The Behavioral Solution

Effective feedback isn't one-size-fits-all. Behavior is shaped by consequences—but only when those consequences are delivered in ways the performer can respond to. That means the power of feedback lies not just in *what* is said, but *how*, *when*, and *to whom* it's delivered.

To make feedback effective across individuals, leaders must adapt their delivery style, timing, and frequency based on the needs of the performer. This isn't about coddling—it's about precision. It requires observation, active listening, and a willingness to test and adjust. When feedback is matched to the performer's learning history, current context, and motivation, it becomes a shaping tool. When it's mismatched, it becomes noise—or worse, a punisher.

DO THIS → NOT THAT

So how do you make that actionable—how do you operationalize it? Start by replacing one-size-fits-all feedback habits with behaviorally sound alternatives. Here's how:

Do This

Ask team members how they prefer to receive feedback
Example: "Would it be more helpful to get quick check-ins in person, or would you prefer written notes after meetings?"

Provide written follow-up for complex feedback
Example: After a dense verbal debrief, the leader sends a short summary email outlining key points and next steps.

Adapt feedback frequency based on experience level
Example: New staff receive daily touchpoints, while experienced team members get weekly check-ins based on need.

Use private, affirming corrections when someone is feedback-sensitive
Example: Pulling someone aside after a tough moment to say, "I know that was frustrating. Let's talk through how to handle that next time."

Match feedback examples to the person's goals and context

Example: "You said you want to move into a leadership role— documenting your process like this helps show initiative and decision-making."

Not That

Assume everyone prefers public recognition

Example: Announcing praise in front of the team without knowing if that person values public attention or finds it uncomfortable.

Deliver dense feedback verbally and walk away

Example: Giving a five-minute monologue of performance feedback without checking for understanding or offering follow-up.

Give all team members the same feedback schedule

Example: "We do feedback every Friday for everyone," regardless of performance or context.

Deliver critique in front of the group to "make a point"

Example: Correcting a team member's mistake during a meeting with others present as a warning to the group.

Speak generically without connecting to their motivators

Example: "Good job with that task," with no reference to what matters to the performer or how it connects to their goals.

SUMMARY

Feedback is only as good as the behavior it shapes. And shaping behavior requires precision—not just in what we say, but in how we say it, when we say it, and to whom.

When feedback is mismatched, even the most well-meaning input can backfire. However, when it's tailored to the performer, feedback becomes a personalized roadmap to success. As a leader, your role is to deliver feedback in a way that produces meaningful behavior change. That's the difference between feedback that checks a box and feedback that drives performance.

Key Takeaways:

➤ Not all feedback works for all people. Match the delivery to the learner.

➤ Behavior is selected by consequences—but only if the feedback is received and processed.

➤ Feedback should set the occasion for future success—not suppress effort through punishment.

➤ Learning histories, preferences, and context matter. Adapt accordingly.

➤ Asking how someone likes feedback is a leadership behavior—not a weakness.

One-size feedback doesn't fit all. But the right fit? That changes everything.

CHAPTER 6

RECOGNITION WITHOUT REINFORCEMENT FALLS FLAT

HOW TO TURN RECOGNITION INTO REAL RESULTS

There's no shortage of celebrations in most organizations—employee of the month plaques, high-five emails, pizza parties for hitting quarterly targets. But if you've ever given someone a shoutout, only to see their performance plateau or decline, you've probably experienced this truth: not all recognition is reinforcing.

Recognition, when done right, can supercharge behavior. But when done wrong—or disconnected from meaningful contingencies—it falls flat. In fact, it can even backfire. The science of behavior teaches us that only *reinforcement* increases the future likelihood of behavior. And not everything labeled as recognition meets that standard.

What's the Behavioral Challenge?

Many well-meaning leaders confuse recognition with reinforcement. They assume that as long as they say something nice or offer a reward, performance will improve. But behavior doesn't work that way. If there's no clear contingency—no observable relationship between the behavior and the outcome—recognition becomes noise.

Even worse, what leaders intend as recognition can function as a punisher. Imagine a reserved employee being called out in front of the entire company. While the intention was appreciation, the result might be embarrassment and withdrawal.

The behavioral truth? Reinforcement *always* works—if it's delivered correctly. When you don't see behavior increasing, it's not that reinforcement failed—it's that what you delivered wasn't preferred *by that person*.

This chapter unpacks why empty recognition doesn't sustain behavior, how to distinguish between rewards and reinforcers, and how to use data—not just good intentions—to guide what actually works.

The Behavioral Indicators

When recognition lacks contingency—meaning it isn't clearly tied to a specific behavior or followed by improved performance—it becomes just another box to check. In these cases, what's labeled as "feedback" is often little more than surface-level praise, not producing meaningful change. Leaders may feel like they're doing their part by offering thanks or throwing a celebration, but performers experience it as empty or irrelevant, especially when it doesn't align with what actually motivates them. These mismatches stall performance and can actively damage trust, create confusion, and undermine morale.

In both leader and performer behavior, we can spot the breakdown. The leader's signals become non-contingent—delivered regardless of whether the behavior met expectations or not—which strips the feedback of its meaning and confuses the performer. Signals may also become inconsistent or even punishing. The performer, in turn, stops connecting effort to outcomes—because, frankly, there is no visible outcome.

Leader Behavior:

- Offers the same form of praise to everyone regardless of effort or impact

  Example: A manager gives generic "great job" messages in every staff meeting without connecting it to specific behavior. Over time, team members stop paying attention.

- Celebrates outcomes without identifying contributing behaviors

  Example: A leader praises a team for hitting a sales goal but doesn't call out the consistent follow-up calls that got them there.

- Focuses on group-level rewards with no individual contingency

  Example: Everyone gets a bonus, even those who underperformed, leading high performers to question the value of extra effort.

- Uses public recognition without considering individual preferences

  Example: An introverted analyst gets called on stage at a company event and avoids volunteering again.

- Reinforces behavior too long after

  Example: Recognition for a completed project comes three months after delivery—long after the behavior that earned it has faded.

Performer Behavior:

- Shows indifference to recognition efforts

  Example: A high performer receives a gift card and says thanks—but their effort doesn't increase or sustain.

- Appears embarrassed or uncomfortable after public praise

  Example: After being publicly thanked, a team member starts arriving late to avoid team meetings.

- Questions the fairness or meaning of recognition

  Example: An employee remarks, "Everyone gets these awards, so they don't really mean anything."

- Becomes less engaged following a recognition moment

  Example: A project manager receives a generic "Employee of the Month" email blast—then quietly withdraws from future stretch projects.

- Shifts motivation from the work to the reward itself

  Example: A performer begins asking, "Do we get anything for this?" before committing effort, indicating a shift away from intrinsic value.

These indicators show that something's off—not necessarily in what's being said, but in how and why it's delivered.

The Behavioral Science Behind the Behavior

Reinforcement, in behavior science, is not about what we *intend*—it's about the *effect* on future behavior. If the behavior doesn't increase or sustain, it wasn't reinforcing. Full stop.

This is why we differentiate between rewards and reinforcers. A **reward** is something given with the hope that it feels good or is appreciated. A **reinforcer** is something that actually increases the future probability of the behavior it follows. The difference lies in the *impact*, not the intent.

So how do we determine what's reinforcing? We look at the data:

- Did the behavior increase or maintain?
- Did the person seek out opportunities to engage in it again?

- Did the environment become more behaviorally rich as a result?

We also need to remember that preferences aren't reinforcers—not until they show impact. A person might *say* they like verbal praise, but if their behavior doesn't change after receiving it, then it wasn't a reinforcer in that context. Preferences are where we start—but impact is how we know.

And while many organizations rely on extrinsic rewards, they often ignore the naturally occurring reinforcers that exist in the work itself: autonomy, mastery, connection, progress, contribution. Leaders who understand how to tie feedback to *these* reinforcers create sustainable performance—not just momentary bursts.

Finally, reinforcement must be *contingent*. That means it should follow the specific behavior you want to see again—and the performer should be able to recognize that connection. If the dots aren't connected, reinforcement can't do its job.

The Behavioral Solution

Recognition only becomes reinforcement when it changes behavior. That means it's not about how *you* feel delivering it—

it's about what *happens next*. Too often, well-meaning praise falls flat because it's misaligned, mistimed, or simply unearned. True reinforcement isn't generic—it's strategic. It's rooted in observable behavior, tailored to the individual, and tested by its effects. If performance isn't sustained or improved, then the recognition didn't reinforce—it may have even punished.

This section focuses on shaping behavior with intention. Recognition, when aligned with reinforcement principles, becomes one of the most powerful tools in a leader's toolbox. It works by increasing the likelihood of behaviors that produce meaningful outcomes—such as problem-solving, collaboration, initiative, and precision. Recognition strengthens patterns of performance that support the goals and values of the organization. Here's how to make that happen:

- **Start with the behavior, not the person.** What did they *do* that added value? Reinforce that.

- **Identify reinforcers through observation and data.** What do people seek out? What gets their attention? What sustains their effort?

- **Deliver reinforcement as close to the behavior as possible.** Timing matters. Immediate feedback is more powerful than delayed accolades.

- **Ensure the reinforcement is contingent.** Don't give out praise or rewards unless it's earned. Otherwise, you dilute the value.

- **Check the impact.** If the behavior doesn't increase, what you thought was reinforcing... wasn't. Adjust.

DO THIS → NOT THAT

Generic recognition may come from good intentions, but if it's not shaping behavior, it's not doing its job. That's why leaders need to distinguish between performative praise and strategic reinforcement. Below are common missteps to avoid—and what to do instead if you want feedback that drives performance.

Do This

Say: "Your follow-up emails after each call directly impacted the client saying yes."
This links the praise to a specific, value-added behavior.

Ask: "Would you rather be recognized in private or at the next team meeting?"
This honors individual reinforcement preferences.

Track behavior post-recognition to assess whether it had an effect.

Use data to confirm whether the reinforcement is increasing the target behavior.

Use a reinforcement survey or brief preference assessment to identify what's most meaningful.
Example: "Quick check—do you prefer time off, public shoutouts, or extra responsibilities?"

Deliver feedback the same day the performance occurs.
Timely feedback strengthens the behavior-consequence connection.

Not That

Say: "Thanks for all you do."
This vague praise doesn't tell the performer what to keep doing.

Assume everyone likes public recognition.
Some may find it uncomfortable or even punishing.

Rely on pizza parties as your only form of acknowledgment.
Group rewards may not function as reinforcement for individual behavior.

Give generic rewards without tying them to behavior.
Example: "Here's a gift card," with no mention of what it's for.

Praise someone weeks after the behavior happened.

The link between behavior and outcome is lost.

SUMMARY

Recognition without reinforcement is like clapping for an actor who's already left the stage. It might feel good, but it does nothing to shape future performance.

To create a feedback culture that sustains growth, leaders must stop treating recognition as a one-size-fits-all perk—and start treating it as a behavior-shaping tool. That means anchoring recognition in behavior, tailoring it to individual reinforcers, and assessing whether it *actually works*.

In behavior science, there's no such thing as a neutral consequence. It either helps or it hinders. And when it comes to performance, empty celebration does more harm than good.

Reinforcement isn't optional. It's how behavior works. The better we get at delivering it, the more likely we are to build a team that performs—not for applause, but because the work itself becomes worth doing again.

CHAPTER 7

LEADING THROUGH FEEDBACK DURING CRISIS

HOW TO LEVERAGE FEEDBACK TO ANCHOR STABILITY AND DIRECTION WHEN THE STAKES ARE HIGH

When a storm hits—whether it's a sudden organizational change, a high-stakes error, or an external crisis—the natural tendency for many leaders is to go quiet, retreat to planning mode, or react with command-and-control behavior. The thinking goes: "Let's just get through this," and communication becomes scarce, inconsistent, or overly reactive. Ironically, this is when people need feedback most. Not empty reassurances or vague check-ins, but clear, calm, consistent information that helps them anchor their behavior and regain a sense of control.

Crisis magnifies everything. It amplifies uncertainty, narrows focus, and intensifies emotional responses. In this space, feedback does more than shape performance—it shapes psychological stability. When delivered effectively, it can redirect panic into purpose, confusion into clarity, and paralysis into forward motion.

This chapter explores how feedback becomes a stabilizing force in crisis. It's not about sugarcoating or avoiding hard truths. It's about making sure people know what to do, how to do it, and that their behavior still matters—even in the storm.

The Behavioral Challenge

In high-stakes situations, the environment is often flooded with competing **motivating operations (MOs)**—uncertainty, fear, urgency, shifting expectations. These conditions shift how people perceive risk and reward. Without clear feedback, the motivational landscape leans toward escape and avoidance. People are less likely to initiate, innovate, or ask for help. Instead, they hunker down—or check out.

This is where many leaders unintentionally punish effort. In the chaos, they ignore small wins, focus on what's broken, or deliver blunt corrections with no support. The result? Disengagement, confusion, and increased stress behavior—like micromanagement, missed deadlines, or interpersonal friction.

Behaviorally, this is a crisis in contingency clarity. In uncertain environments, people need clear, immediate feedback to know whether their actions are helping or hurting. Without it, the natural reinforcing properties of progress, mastery, or connection are lost in the noise.

The Behavioral Indicators

A crisis doesn't change the principles of behavior—it intensifies them. The behaviors of both leaders and performers become sharper indicators of the feedback system's strength or weakness. I once worked with an organization that hit a sudden funding shortfall. The leader, instead of panicking or going silent, doubled down on transparent, timely feedback. They acknowledged uncertainty but consistently reinforced small wins—recognizing initiative, effort, and collaboration in real time. Not only did the team stay engaged, they rallied. On the flip side, I've seen leaders disappear during a crisis, offering little guidance and no recognition. And in that silence, high performers drifted, low performers disengaged, and culture collapsed under the weight of uncertainty.

Leader Behavior:

- Withdraws communication or becomes overly directive

  Example: A school principal cancels all team meetings during a crisis but starts sending rigid daily memos with step-by-step instructions. Staff feel micromanaged and isolated, unsure where they stand or how to contribute.

- Avoids acknowledging team stress or emotional impact

  Example: During a chaotic rollout, a clinic director jumps straight into logistics and deadlines without addressing staff exhaustion or emotional strain. Morale drops, and quiet resentment builds.

- Delivers only negative feedback or urgent commands

  Example: A department head sends multiple urgent emails in ALL CAPS demanding updates but offers no recognition for staff pulling late nights. Stress increases, but direction and reinforcement are absent.

- Fails to reinforce small but critical wins

  Example: A project manager ignores a team member's effort to troubleshoot a system failure, focusing only on what still needs to be fixed. The lack of reinforcement flattens motivation in the moment it's needed most.

- Ignores input or dismisses questions

  Example: A staff member raises a concern during a crisis debrief, and the leader replies, "We don't have time for that right now." The message is clear: compliance matters more than collaboration.

Performer Behavior:

- Becomes reactive or overly cautious

  Example: A team member begins double- and triple-checking every decision before acting, slowing down progress out of fear of being wrong or reprimanded.

- Stops offering ideas or asking for clarification

  Example: A marketing associate used to contribute fresh ideas in meetings. After repeated shutdowns during a high-pressure campaign, she stays silent and nods along—even when she sees issues.

- Displays increased errors or slower response times

  Example: A behavior technician starts making documentation mistakes and takes longer to respond to clients during peak hours. The stress and lack of clear guidance interfere with performance.

- Exhibits emotional outbursts or passive withdrawal

  Example: An employee lashes out in frustration during a team call—then turns off their camera and says nothing for the rest of the meeting. The pattern repeats in the days that follow.

- Focuses on avoiding mistakes rather than achieving goals

  Example: A normally proactive nurse stops initiating patient care solutions during a staffing crisis. She's been corrected harshly in public during past emergencies, so now she waits for explicit instructions before acting—even when time matters.

Together, these behaviors suggest a breakdown in psychological safety and behavioral alignment. From a behavioral perspective, psychological safety means that individuals feel their actions won't be met with punishment, ridicule, or exclusion, which creates a supportive environment where they can take risks, seek feedback, and learn. Without reinforcing, directional feedback, that sense of safety erodes—leading to erratic behavior during a crisis and a decline in performance under conditions that allow for errors to magnify exponentially.

The Behavioral Science Behind the Behavior

From a behavioral lens, crisis increases motivating operations—particularly aversive ones. The environment signals threat, and escape or avoidance behavior becomes more likely. If the leader's behavior adds to the aversive conditions (e.g., through blame, silence, or inconsistency), even high-performing staff may shut down.

Reinforcement and punishment don't stop working in crisis—they become more potent. Unfortunately, well-meaning leaders often misapply feedback under pressure. They delay reinforcement ("I'll recognize them when this is over"), rely on vague generalities ("We just need everyone to step up"), or deliver punitive corrections without a pathway forward.

The science is clear: under stress, the brain narrows its focus to immediate consequences. Think about it—when was the last time something startled or scared you? Your behavior probably shifted fast, focused on escape or resolution, not reflection. In those moments, we respond to what's right in front of us. That's why feedback must be clear, directional, and reinforcing in the moment. Behavior science gives leaders the tools to shape effective responses—especially under pressure, when clarity and reinforcement matter most.

The Behavioral Solution

In a crisis, people benefit from clarity, grounding, and reinforcement. When the stakes are high, feedback becomes a critical tool for stabilizing performance. It's most effective when it reduces ambiguity, acknowledges effort, and guides behavior toward actionable outcomes.

From a behavioral perspective, feedback in a crisis must serve three distinct functions:

- **Anchor** people to shared values that give meaning to their actions.

- **Direct** them with specific behaviors that lead to safety, efficiency, or resolution.

- **Reinforce** progress—especially the small wins that might otherwise go unnoticed amid the chaos.

Crisis amplifies emotion, narrows attention, and shifts priorities, making behavior less stable and more likely to be shaped by environmental cues like your tone, timing, and presence..

Here's how to ensure your feedback anchors, directs, and reinforces when your people need it most:

- **Anchor behavior in shared values.** Remind people of the purpose behind their work.

Example: "Your quick action this morning prevented a much bigger issue. That's leadership under pressure."

- **Direct behavior toward clear, achievable steps.** Give them something concrete to do, not just something abstract to aim for.

  Example: "Let's make sure we're checking the med carts before every round. It'll save us time and reduce stress later."

- **Reinforce consistency and effort, not just outcomes.** Even small wins deserve attention when energy is low.

  Example: "I saw how calmly you handled that parent call. That steadiness is what keeps us grounded."

DO THIS → NOT THAT

When tension runs high, it's easy to default to commands, blame, or vague encouragement. But in a crisis, those approaches can trigger stress responses, shut down problem-solving, and widen the gap between leaders and their teams. The key is to replace emotional reactions with behaviorally sound responses. Using behavior science supports people in meeting expectations— even when the world feels unstable.

Here are five common feedback missteps during crisis—and how to replace them with more effective alternatives:

Do This

Prioritize critical behaviors tied to immediate goals
Example: "Let's focus only on what impacts safety today—everything else can wait."

Reinforce effort and small wins as soon as possible
Example: "Thanks for staying calm during that tough moment—your composure helped the team stay grounded."

Address issues privately with corrective support
Example: "Let's step aside and talk through what happened so we can reset without the group watching."

Acknowledge the emotional toll while reinforcing effort
Example: "I know this has been draining—but I see how hard you're pushing forward, and that matters."

Clarify 1–2 priority behaviors and explain why they matter now
Example: "Right now, the most important thing is clear documentation. It helps us protect clients and make fast decisions."

Not That

Make vague, pressure-filled demands

Example: "Everyone needs to work harder."

Delay praise until the crisis feels distant or disconnected

Example: Waiting days or weeks to acknowledge behavior after a high-pressure event, when the moment—and the motivation— has already passed.

Criticize mistakes publicly

Example: Calling out an error in a staff meeting to "set an example."

Ignore team stress or burnout

Example: Pushing ahead with tasks and expectations without recognizing the emotional weight of the situation.

Assume people know what matters

Example: Offering no guidance during shifting priorities and expecting people to intuit what to focus on.

This isn't about sugarcoating reality. It's about reinforcing the behaviors that will carry people—and the mission—through it.

SUMMARY

Crisis reveals more than it creates. It exposes the strength of a feedback culture and the systems that shape behavior under pressure. In these moments, leaders serve as behavioral anchors—stabilizing action through what they say, how they say it, and when they say it.

Effective feedback during crisis:

- Reduces ambiguity
- Reinforces alignment
- Protects emotional bandwidth
- Sustains performance under stress

Strong leaders use feedback to anchor behavior in shared values, direct behavior toward actionable steps, and reinforce effort and consistency when it matters most. So, when the pressure's on, stay present. Reinforce. Direct. Lead. One clear piece of feedback at a time.

CHAPTER 8

WHEN FEEDBACK FAILS—
THE BREAKDOWN OF THE LOOP

WHAT YOU DON'T SAY STILL SENDS A MESSAGE

Imagine a team meeting where your message lands with a thud. You roll out new expectations, offer a few reminders about priorities, and close with a vague, "let's stay on top of things." You've said your part—but later that week, nothing has changed. Deadlines are still missed. Communication gaps persist. And you wonder, "Did they even hear me?"

Chapter 1 established why feedback is essential to shaping performance. This chapter examines what happens when feedback fails—specifically, how breakdowns in the feedback loop lead to disconnects between behavior and results. Feedback functions as a loop, and when that loop breaks, the connection between actions and outcomes weakens.

What's the Behavioral Challenge?

It's not just about giving feedback—it's about whether feedback loops are functioning. Many leaders *think* they're giving feedback, but their message doesn't land. Why? Because the loop is broken. There's no observable consequence following the behavior, or the feedback never comes at all. Without a functioning loop, people are left guessing.

When feedback is missing altogether, behavior begins to drift. People fill in the blanks based on their own assumptions. High performers assume they're doing fine and keep doing what they've always done. Underperformers assume their behavior is acceptable. Many team members interpret the silence as indifference. *If you don't say anything, you must not care.* Over time, the absence of feedback weakens alignment, erodes trust, and allows performance to shift off course.

Leaders might mistakenly think silence is neutral, but behaviorally, it's not. The absence of feedback is still feedback. When the loop is broken, people operate in the dark—guessing at what matters, unsure of what's working, and slowly detaching from the behaviors that drive value. The result? Performance plateaus or declines, and morale begins to erode.

The Behavioral Indicators

To recognize broken feedback loops, look at how they show up in observable behavior. A healthy feedback loop depends on continuity, responsiveness, and reinforcement. When any part of that loop breaks, both leader and performer behavior shift in predictable—and often costly—ways.

Below are signs that the feedback loop is no longer functioning—and real-world examples that show how these patterns play out:

Leader Behavior:

- Fails to acknowledge key performance moments
  Example: A team member solves a customer complaint on their own using an innovative workaround. Their manager witnesses it but says nothing, missing an opportunity to reinforce initiative and problem-solving.

- Repeats expectations with no reference to past behavior
  Example: During every staff meeting, a supervisor says, "Remember to document client notes the same day." But they never acknowledge when it's done right—or when it's missed—so the reminder becomes white noise.

- Fails to follow up on previous conversations

  Example: A leader gives feedback on presentation skills and agrees to revisit the topic in two weeks. A month passes with no mention of it again. The performer wonders if it even mattered.

- Waits for formal reviews to address issues

  Example: A supervisor notices repeated issues with punctuality but avoids discussing them until the annual review. By then, the behavior has become ingrained—and the delayed correction feels punitive.

Performer Behavior:

- Continues undesired behavior with no change

  Example: An employee keeps turning in reports late. Since there's no acknowledgment or correction, they assume it's not an issue—or that nobody notices.

- Asks fewer questions or stops seeking input

  Example: A team member used to check in weekly to make sure they were on track. Now they don't bother. Previous attempts to get feedback were met with vague answers or silence.

- Appears disengaged, uncertain, or unmotivated

  Example: A once-enthusiastic new hire starts showing up late to meetings, avoids volunteering, and offers one-word updates. It's not laziness—it's a reaction to operating in a feedback vacuum.

- Makes assumptions about what's acceptable

  Example: Without feedback, a performer begins creating their own "rules of engagement." They take liberties with deadlines, messaging tone, or decision-making authority—simply because boundaries were never reinforced.

These behaviors reveal a deeper disconnect: the feedback loop has broken down completely. Without consistent input and observable consequences, neither party has the information needed to adjust. The system becomes static—driven by silence, assumptions, and a lack of meaningful reinforcement.

Consider a senior analyst who stops submitting new proposals after their recent efforts don't receive a response. They cannot observe any meaningful impact from their behavior. Similarly, a customer service rep continues making the same mistakes because no one provided corrective feedback. When feedback is absent, behavior stalls and begins to drift.

The Behavioral Science Behind the Behavior

From a behavior science perspective, feedback connects actions to consequences. When that connection is missing, behavior extinguishes or becomes erratic. This is a failure of what we call contingency clarity.

If the consequence—feedback—doesn't clearly follow the behavior, the learning is lost. If there is no consequence at all, behavior loses its functional anchor. People either keep doing what they've always done or start allocating behavior elsewhere—often in ways that produce outcomes in other environments.

Human behavior—like all organism behavior—is shaped by consequences. Just as species adapt over generations by developing traits that support survival and reproduction, individuals allocate behavior moment by moment based on what pays off. Consequences select behavior in milliseconds, minutes, hours, and days. Immediate reinforcement keeps behavior moving. Ultimate consequences—like success, trust, or growth—are only reachable when people can track what behaviors get them there.

Remember that as leaders, we are integral parts of the environment. More precisely, we are the arrangers of the environment. Unlike species in nature that cannot change their surroundings, leaders have the ability to design environments that positively influence behavior. The higher you are in the organization, the greater your capacity to shape these environments. Feedback plays a central role—it is the fastest, clearest, and most accessible way to connect behavior to results.

The Behavioral Solution

When feedback loops break down, the path forward isn't more noise—it's more precision. Closing the loop requires leaders to deliver feedback that is **clear, timely,** and **connected to meaningful outcomes**. But it also requires a shift in mindset: feedback isn't something you do to someone—it's something you build with them.

That means we don't just broadcast directives and hope for the best. We check for understanding, reinforce what's working, and correct with care. More importantly, *we* do it often and with purpose—because every missed opportunity to reinforce performance is a missed opportunity to shape it.

THE FEEDBACK EFFECT | Dr. Paul Gavoni

DO THIS → NOT THAT

To repair a failing feedback system, leaders must apply these strategies—and understand the science behind them:

Do This

Specify the exact behavior that needs to change—or continue
Example: "In your last report, the executive summary was missing key data points from the third quarter. Including those next time will make the report more actionable for leadership."

Deliver feedback as close to the performance as possible
Example: "The way you de-escalated that situation with Marcus—calm tone, clear directions, and giving him a minute to reset—was exactly what we needed in that moment."

Tie feedback to natural reinforcers that matter to the performer
Example: "By including the tracking codes up front, you're saving the team hours in back-end sorting. That's helping everyone hit their deadlines faster."

Check for understanding and invite input to build buy-in
Example: "We've talked about increasing client follow-ups. What do you think would help make that easier on your end?"

Not That

Say "Do better" or "That needs work."

Example: Offering vague criticism without pointing to a specific behavior or result.

Wait days or weeks to give feedback

Example: Praising or correcting someone weeks after the behavior occurred, when the learning window has closed.

Rely on vague praise like, "Great job."

Example: Offering generic praise that doesn't explain what was effective or why it mattered.

Give one-way feedback without dialogue

Example: Delivering feedback as a directive, without asking questions or encouraging reflection.

Closing the Loop with the 4 Cs

Even well-intended feedback can fall flat without structure. Effective leaders shape behavior by delivering feedback anchored in observable actions, meaningful consequences, and consistent reinforcement. To make feedback stick and rebuild trust in a broken system, leaders can apply a simple but powerful framework: the 4 Cs of effective feedback. This approach turns feedback into a system, not a guess, ensuring every message drives clarity, consistency, context, and credibility.

Think of each feedback opportunity as a chance to install these four behavioral anchors:

- **Clarity** – *What exactly should they do?*
  → "Double-check the billing codes before submitting the report."

- **Consistency** – *Do you give feedback often and predictably?*
  → "Each week during check-ins, let's look at two wins and one area for adjustment."

- **Context** – *Why does the behavior matter?*
  → "Submitting reports early gives our admin team more time to troubleshoot issues before the client sees them."

- **Credibility** – *Are you reinforcing real behaviors or just reacting emotionally?*
  → "I've seen you stay late to work on the project three days this week to cover gaps. That level of commitment makes a difference to this team—and I want you to know I see it."

SUMMARY

So, what should leaders take away from the breakdown of the feedback loop?

When feedback fails, it reflects a leadership performance issue. These breakdowns in the loop are often quiet, subtle, and easy to miss. Their impact, however, is significant. That's why leaders must treat feedback as a daily behavior-shaping practice rather than an optional add-on.

As you reflect on your own feedback habits, ask yourself: Is your feedback looping back? Are you providing input that's timely, actionable, and visible? Are you checking to see how it lands?

Because without that loop, behavior loses its way—and performance suffers.

Here's what to remember:

▸ Feedback loops break down when input is missing, delayed, or ignored.

▸ Silence breeds assumption—and assumption erodes accountability.

▸ You are part of the environment. But more importantly, you're the architect of it.

> ➤ Effective leadership evolves feedback beyond basic messaging, creating a system that intentionally shapes performance.

And like any system, it only works when the loop stays closed.

CHAPTER 9

CORRECTION THAT BUILDS, NOT BREAKS

BUILDING PERFORMANCE WITHOUT BREAKING RELATIONSHIPS

Most people don't like corrective feedback. And honestly: Who can blame them?

In too many organizations, it's overused, poorly delivered, or worse—weaponized. People are corrected for behaviors they were never trained to do well in the first place. Or the feedback comes after long stretches of silence, building resentment instead of behavior. In these environments, correction becomes something to fear, not something to grow from.

But it doesn't have to be that way.

When delivered with intention and supported by positive reinforcement, corrective feedback becomes a tool for growth. The key lies in how, when, and why it's delivered. When leaders consistently reinforce effort, highlight incremental gains, and maintain a 4:1 ratio of positive to corrective interactions, feedback feels like guidance—not punishment.

And it all starts with trust.

If the relationship isn't there, the feedback won't land. Trust turns correction from a threat into a signal: "I see your potential, and I care enough to help you meet it."

This chapter explores the science of delivering corrective feedback that shapes performance while preserving relationships. When delivered effectively, corrective feedback becomes a valued tool for growth.

The Behavioral Challenge

Let's call it what it is: many leaders avoid correction until it's too late. They let missteps pile up, hoping things will improve on their own. Then, when frustration boils over, they correct in a way that's harsh, vague, or emotionally charged. The result? Defensiveness. Disengagement. Sometimes even defiance.

The science is clear: feedback must be timely, specific, and tied to a clear standard. Delaying correction—or delivering it inconsistently—creates ambiguity. And ambiguity kills performance. It's also important to recognize that corrective feedback, by its very nature, is aversive. That means it must be used carefully and sparingly. When overused, it stops teaching and starts punishing.

Leaders must ask: Am I using correction to shape growth? Or am I just expressing frustration?

The Behavioral Indicators

When corrective feedback is misused or delivered without a foundation of trust and reinforcement, its effects ripple through the organization. The signs are visible in people's behavior. Leaders may begin reacting rather than guiding, avoiding difficult conversations or defaulting to frustration. Performers often disengage, become defensive, or repeat mistakes because they haven't been taught what to do differently. When feedback doesn't function as instruction, motivation declines and performance suffers. These indicators serve as data points showing that the system requires adjustment.

Leader Behavior:

- Avoids addressing performance issues until they escalate
  Example: A supervisor stays silent for weeks, then unloads a list of grievances in one sitting.

- Focuses on what went wrong, not how to fix it
  Example: "You keep missing deadlines!" without offering strategies or support.

- Uses tone, body language, or timing that adds aversive properties
  Example: Providing feedback in front of peers or during moments of high stress.

- Delivers feedback inconsistently or arbitrarily
  Example: Sometimes corrects, sometimes ignores, leaving the performer guessing.

- Doesn't check for understanding or allow for reflection
  Example: Delivers the feedback and walks away, assuming agreement.

Performer Behavior:

- Reacts defensively or shuts down

  Example: Responds with excuses, withdrawal, or visible frustration.

- Avoids tasks or situations tied to previous correction

  Example: Stops volunteering for projects after being publicly corrected.

- Asks fewer questions or becomes less communicative

  Example: Begins "playing it safe" to avoid further critique.

- Does not improve performance after feedback

  Example: Repeats the same errors due to lack of clarity or support.

- Exhibits signs of stress, disengagement, or burnout

  Example: Increased absenteeism, missed deadlines, or low energy.

These signals point to a deeper issue: feedback that doesn't function as instruction. And if it's not building behavior, it's breaking it.

THE FEEDBACK EFFECT | Dr. Paul Gavoni

The Behavioral Science Behind the Behavior

As you've learned, feedback doesn't play just one role. While it's often talked about as an *antecedent*—something that sets the occasion for future behavior—it can also serve other functions depending on how and when it's delivered. Sometimes it is a consequence that reinforces behavior after it happens. Other times, it acts as a signal that tells someone what behaviors are likely to be rewarded moving forward (remember a *discriminative stimulus*—a cue that tells someone, "If you do X right now, good things will follow").

That's why understanding the *function* of feedback—what it actually does in the moment—is more important than simply giving it. When feedback is misused, it can confuse, discourage, or even punish. When it's used well, it becomes one of the most powerful leadership tools available.

Corrective feedback, by itself, doesn't teach. It alerts. It tells someone something was off, but it doesn't show them how to get it right. That's where many leaders go wrong: they stop at the correction. Sustainable behavior change happens when leaders guide people toward the right behavior—and then reinforce their progress.

Effective corrective feedback should:

- **Be immediate** – The closer feedback is delivered to the behavior, the more likely it is to be connected and useful.

- **Be specific** – Vague feedback like "you need to do better" doesn't help. Call out exactly what needs to change.

- **Include a clear alternative** – Don't just say what not to do—explain or model what to do instead.

- **Be backed by reinforcement** – Feedback alone won't build fluency. Reinforcement—acknowledging effort, celebrating progress, rewarding improvement—must be part of the system.

Behavioral science reminds us: growth happens through *shaping*—reinforcing small improvements over time. So don't wait for perfection. Break performance down into teachable steps, celebrate the wins along the way, and build a culture where correction is helpful, not harmful.

The Behavioral Solution

Corrective feedback should focus on helping people improve by building skills and confidence to perform effectively. In many workplaces, correction functions as discipline rather than development. It tends to be reactive, emotional, and sporadic, often occurring without a foundation of trust or positive reinforcement. That kind of feedback shuts people down as opposed to shaping behavior toward desired goals.

If the goal is to improve performance—not just punish errors— corrective feedback must be delivered with care, consistency, and behavioral precision. It should feel like guidance that builds momentum within a larger system of support, where successes are reinforced far more often than mistakes are called out. A strong relationship is fundamental to this process. Trust provides the foundation that allows feedback to have real impact and foster growth. Effective feedback depends on connection, clarity, and consistency.

Correction is not a one-time conversation—it's a continuous leadership practice. Here's how to deliver correction that supports performance and strengthens your team:

Check the Conditions Before You Correct

- Have you reinforced this person's behavior recently?

- Do they know what "right" looks like?

Are you correcting behavior—or venting emotion?

Use a 3-Part Feedback Formula

1. **Observe**: "I noticed you…"

2. **Impact:** "That created…"

3. **Next Step:** "Next time, try…"

Example: "I noticed you skipped the pre-check before submitting the proposal. That led to some formatting errors the client flagged. Next time, let's use the checklist together—want to take 5 minutes now?"

Prompt Reflection, Don't Just Prescribe

Ask questions like:

- "How do you think that went?"

- "What felt off to you?"

- "What might we try differently next time?"

These promote ownership and engagement—not just compliance.

Follow Up with Positive Reinforcement

Remember, the goal is to maintain a 4:1 ratio of recognizing good performance to correcting errors. When the person improves—even slightly—catch it.

Example: "You paused to double-check the client list today. That extra step kept things tight—great adjustment."

That's how you close the loop and build momentum.

DON'T DO THIS → DO THIS INSTEAD

Corrective feedback is effective only when it produces the desired behavior. This requires delivering the message in a way that supports change. Vague criticism, delayed conversations, and emotional outbursts often lead to defensive performers, broken trust, and behaviors that fail to improve or even worsen.

Effective corrective feedback is timely, behavior-specific, and delivered in a way that protects the relationship while pointing the performer toward growth. It avoids personal attacks and focuses on what can be done differently next time. Below are common missteps to avoid—and what to do instead to ensure your corrective feedback leads to real, lasting improvement.

Do This

Deliver corrective feedback early, calmly, and consistently

Example: "Let's talk through that now while it's fresh—here's what I noticed and what we can adjust next time."

Describe the desired behavior and how to get there

Example: "Instead of skipping the safety check, make it part of your pre-shift routine. It'll save time and reduce risk."

Provide feedback privately and during low-stress moments

Example: "Can we step aside for a quick debrief? I want to walk through that calmly."

Assess whether the behavior was ever clearly taught or reinforced

Example: "Let's revisit this together—if we didn't model it clearly, that's on us too."

Reinforce any step in the right direction

Example: "That's a big improvement from last time—keep going in that direction."

Not That

Wait until frustration builds before giving feedback

Example: Letting issues pile up, then snapping or giving feedback in anger.

Focus only on what went wrong

Example: "That was a mess—don't do it like that again."

Correct in public or during emotionally charged moments

Example: Calling someone out in front of the team when tensions are already high.

Assume the performer "should know better"

Example: "You've been here long enough—you shouldn't need reminders."

Forget to follow up when progress happens

Example: Giving correction but never acknowledging growth afterward.

SUMMARY

Corrective feedback doesn't have to feel like a confrontation. Done well, it's an act of leadership—and a sign of respect. It says, "I believe in you enough to help you grow."

But growth only happens when feedback is safe, specific, and supported. Too many leaders use correction as a hammer. The best is to use it as a chisel—shaping performance one intentional strike at a time.

Ultimately, feedback isn't about pointing out flaws. It's about helping someone become better than they were yesterday. And that's the real legacy of a great leader.

CHAPTER 10

FADING PROMPTS— FROM TELLING TO ASKING

PROMOTING INDEPENDENCE BY PROMPTING THE RIGHT WAY

Most performance issues aren't about not knowing—they're about depending on someone else to think it through. And too often, the problem isn't the performer... it's the prompting.

In well-intentioned attempts to be helpful, leaders often give answers instead of building problem-solvers. They jump in with commands, provide step-by-step directions, or ask questions so leading they may as well be statements. Over time, this creates prompt dependence. Instead of thinking through next steps or evaluating their own behavior, people wait to be told what to do.

That might look like compliance. But it's not competence. And it won't last.

If the goal is sustainable performance—behavior that endures when the leader isn't around—then prompting must be done with intention. The good news? There's a science to it.

Feedback Isn't Just Correction—It's Direction

Before we dive into prompting strategies, it's important to understand where this fits in the broader picture of feedback.

We often think of feedback as something that comes after behavior. But feedback can also function as a prompt—especially when it's specific, immediate, and forward-facing. When we tell someone, "Next time, try this," we're not just responding to the past—we're shaping the future. That's an antecedent.

In that sense, prompting is a form of feedback that sets the stage for behavior before it happens. When done well, it provides just enough guidance to support success—without stealing the opportunity for learning. And like any form of feedback, the goal is not to do it forever. The goal is to fade it—so the performer starts generating their own.

Consider this: Most of us use a GPS—and for good reason. It's a helpful tool for navigating unfamiliar territory. But some people use their GPS to go to the same location repeatedly and still can't get there without it. That's prompt dependence.

Despite repeated experience, they haven't contacted the natural feedback from the environment—landmarks, intersections, timing, or signs—that would allow them to navigate independently. Each step is guided by external input, and that input becomes necessary for performance.

Prompts that were once helpful can become essential—and without them, behavior stalls.

The Behavioral Challenge

In workplace settings, prompt dependence interferes with autonomy, adaptability, and sustained performance. It creates an environment where team members look outward for direction instead of developing the fluency to act based on internal cues and environmental conditions.

This pattern shows up in small ways that add up: repeated reminders, follow-ups, step-by-step instructions, and employees waiting to be told what to do—even for familiar tasks. The more this cycle continues, the less opportunity there is for learning through contact with natural consequences.

Environments that consistently provide direction without a plan for building fluency can suppress problem-solving, delay skill development, and lead to over-reliance on leadership for routine decision-making. In fast-paced or dynamic settings, this results in bottlenecks, missed opportunities, and reduced responsiveness.

Prompting becomes especially problematic when it replaces training, when it's used reactively without data, or when it continues long after the performer is capable of responding independently. Over time, it narrows the performer's repertoire and limits growth.

Prompt dependence is inefficient, unsustainable, and makes the job of the leader exponentially more difficult because of the number of people who may seek them out for support. Without deliberate strategies for fading prompts, leaders may unintentionally reinforce the very behaviors that stall progress.

The Behavioral Indicators

Prompt dependence doesn't always show up as helplessness. It often creeps in subtly—through patterns in how leaders prompt and how performers respond.

Leader Behavior:

- Repeats the same instructions daily

  Example: "Don't forget to check the log"—every single morning.

- Gives answers instead of asking questions

  Example: "Just do it this way"—even when the performer could have figured it out.

- Rushes to prompt before the performer has time to respond

  Example: Interrupts silence with guidance instead of allowing problem-solving.

- Uses leading or directive questions that don't promote thought

  Example: "Wouldn't it make more sense to do X instead?"

Performer Behavior:

- Waits for direction before starting tasks

  Example: Sits idle until told exactly what to do.

- Asks frequent clarification questions on routine procedures

  Example: "Should I use the form again?" for the fifth time that week.

- Shows hesitation or confusion when the leader is unavailable

  Example: Appears stuck or anxious during independent work.

- Struggles to explain the rationale behind their actions

  Example: Can't articulate why they made a certain decision—even if it was correct.

These are all signs that prompting has become a crutch instead of a catalyst. And that calls for a strategic shift.

The Behavioral Science Behind the Behavior

From a behavioral standpoint, prompts are antecedent strategies—signals that increase the likelihood of a behavior. But like any antecedent, prompts must fade over time. If they don't, the behavior stays tethered to the cue instead of transferring to the natural environment.

The key here is that there's a functional difference between telling and asking. Telling delivers the solution. Asking prompts discovery. One builds dependence. The other builds a repertoire. Used correctly, prompts are temporary scaffolds. They exist to support behavior long enough for natural contingencies—

like peer approval, task completion, or reinforcement from success—to take over.

If reinforcement builds behavior, then fading prompts builds ownership.

The Behavioral Solution: Ask, Don't Tell

Prompting is most effective when it supports the development of independent, fluent behavior. That requires a deliberate approach—one that encourages performers to think, reflect, and respond with increasing autonomy.

When leaders use thoughtful questions, they reinforce problem-solving and create space for people to engage more deeply with their own performance. Over time, this approach strengthens internal cues and decision-making skills that transfer across tasks and environments.

To promote independence and reduce unnecessary prompting, leaders can use a structured sequence of questions that gradually shape stronger, more self-directed behavior. This begins by introducing open-ended questions that invite planning and reflection, then narrowing focus as needed to support success.

Use a Prompt Hierarchy of Questioning to build independence:

- **Open-Ended Questions** – Invite analysis and reflection

  "What's your plan for this task?"

- **Focused Questions** – Narrow attention to a key detail

  "What's the first step you need to take?"

- **Leading Questions** – Gently steer without telling

  "Would reviewing the checklist help here?"

- **Directive Questions** – Use only when necessary

  "Can you go log the data now?"

The goal is to stay as high on the hierarchy as possible. Only move down when absolutely necessary—and move back up as soon as you can.

Example of Prompt Fading in Action

Scenario: A staff member frequently forgets to complete a quality assurance step after a task.

- **Week 1 (Directive):** "Don't forget the QA log right after this."

- **Week 2 (Leading):** "What's the last thing you do before finishing the task?"

- **Week 3 (Focused):** "What's your process for wrapping this up?"

- **Week 4 (Open-Ended):** "How do you know everything's complete before moving on?"

Over time, the goal is for the performer to internalize the routine—not rely on you to cue it.

DON'T DO THIS → DO THIS INSTEAD

Prompting is most effective when it's used to build fluency and strengthen independent performance over time. When delivered with intention, prompts help performers access what they already know, apply it to the situation, and become more confident in responding without support.

This approach creates a learning environment where performers are expected to think, reflect, and develop internal cues that guide behavior. Prompts become a tool for growth—one that supports generalization and long-term success beyond the moment.

Here's how intentional prompting shows up in real leadership practice:

Do This

Ask open-ended questions to promote reflection and planning
Example: "What's your plan for handling this?"

Fade prompts using a question hierarchy to strengthen independent performance
Example: Move from directive to focused to open-ended questions over time.

Allow space for silence so the performer can think before responding
Example: Wait a few seconds before prompting if someone hesitates.

Use neutral questions to surface the performer's reasoning
Example: "How did you decide to go that route?"

Build prompting into routines with a plan to fade
Example: "Let's use this checklist for a few weeks and then check for fluency."

Reinforce progress toward fluency and decision-making
Example: "Nice work thinking that through before checking in."

Not That

Deliver the answer immediately

Example: "Just send the follow-up email like we talked about."

Repeat the same prompt each time a task needs to be done

Example: "Don't forget to log the data," day after day.

Jump in too quickly, interrupting problem-solving with a prompt

Example: Giving direction the moment there's a pause.

Use leading questions that signal there's a "right" answer

Example: "Wouldn't it have been better to go the other way?"

Let prompts become permanent without reassessing their function

Example: "I remind them every time because otherwise they forget."

Only praise completion of tasks prompted by you

Example: "Thanks for doing that after I reminded you."

SUMMARY

Prompting, when done with a clear plan and performance focus, strengthens decision-making and supports the development of independent, fluent behavior. The structure of your questions and the timing of your prompts influence whether behavior becomes automatic or remains dependent on external cues.

Leaders who prompt with intention create the conditions for sustainable performance—where people know what to do, how to do it, and when to act without needing to be told.

CHAPTER 11:

DIAGNOSE BEFORE
YOU DELIVER

In the last chapter, we explored how to deliver corrective feedback well. Yet, even when early correction is important, leaders often rush to give feedback the moment performance slips. A missed deadline? "You need to manage your time better." A botched presentation? "Put more effort in next time." But here's the catch: corrective feedback only works when the underlying cause of the issue is behavioral.

And often, it's not.

This chapter is about avoiding costly assumptions and getting curious before getting corrective. Because not all performance problems are truly performance problems. Sometimes, they're leadership problems. Sometimes, they're system problems. And when we diagnose the issue wrong, the intervention backfires.

What's the Behavioral Challenge?

We've all seen it. Leaders who correct behavior that hasn't been taught. Who assume laziness instead of confusion. Who reprimand people for low output when they're drowning in unclear expectations and competing priorities.

Behavior science gives us a simple but critical distinction: is it a "can't do," or a "won't do"?

A "can't do" means the performer lacks the skill, clarity, or tools to meet the expectation. A "won't do" means they're choosing not to engage in the behavior—possibly due to weak reinforcement, competing contingencies, or unclear priorities.

Corrective feedback aimed at a "can't do" doesn't just fail—it often punishes. You're essentially blaming the performer for not doing something they're not yet able to do. Think about it. Imagine your boss giving you corrective feedback for something you aren't yet able to do. For example, being told, "You need to handle client calls better," when you haven't been trained on effective communication skills. This kind of feedback can feel like punishment because it addresses a skill you haven't developed.

That's why effective leaders diagnose before they deliver.

The Behavioral Indicators

Before jumping into feedback, scan for signs that the issue may not be about will—but about skill, clarity, or support. Leaders who rush to correct without assessing these variables risk reinforcing the wrong assumptions and breaking trust. The real insight often lies in the patterns of both leader and performer behavior.

Leader Behavior:

- Assumes all performance gaps are motivation issues
  Example: A manager sees declining report quality and says, "They're just not trying hard enough," without checking whether the performer understands the report structure.

- Delivers correction without confirming fluency or expectations
  Example: A leader corrects a technician for missing steps in a procedure, unaware that they were never properly trained on the updated protocol.

- Provides the same correction repeatedly with no improvement
  Example: A supervisor keeps saying, "Double-check your

work," but never models what that looks like or provides a checklist for reference.

- Fails to assess environmental or systemic contributors
  Example: A team lead criticizes slow response time without noticing that the software system has frequent lags or that the performer has competing priorities.

- Blames the individual instead of evaluating the system
  Example: A principal reprimands a teacher for poor classroom management without reviewing whether they've been trained in behavior strategies or supported by an effective coaching system.

Performer Behavior:

- Appears confused or hesitant during tasks
  Example: A new employee regularly pauses to re-read instructions or ask for help, indicating they haven't yet mastered the workflow.

- Repeats errors even after correction
  Example: A team member continues to submit reports in the wrong format, not out of defiance, but because the instructions were verbal and unclear.

- Seems disengaged or overloaded

  Example: A clinician starts skipping documentation or missing appointments—not from apathy, but because their caseload doubled and they weren't given tools to manage it.

- Expresses uncertainty about expectations

  Example: A staff member asks, "Are we supposed to do this every day?" showing that performance standards haven't been clearly communicated.

- Temporarily improves, then regresses

  Example: After receiving feedback, an employee performs better for a week—then slides back. The feedback may have lacked reinforcement, clarity, or system support.

The Behavioral Science Behind the Behavior

As you've learned, behavior is shaped by antecedents and consequences—what comes before and after. But if you don't understand the function of the behavior, you risk selecting the wrong tool to address it.

Corrective feedback is designed to signal a need for change. But signaling only works if the performer has the means to respond.

If they don't have the skill, clarity, or support, the correction becomes frustrating noise.

The "can't do vs. won't do" distinction is grounded in the science of behavior:

- "Can't do" problems are typically skill deficits, unclear expectations, or lack of environmental support—these require training, modeling, prompting, and system changes.

- "Won't do" problems often result from weak or inconsistent consequences, competing priorities, or a lack of motivation—these may require reinforcement, simplification, or re-alignment with values.

Put simply: correction isn't the cure-all. It's the "last step," not the first.

The Behavioral Solution

Before delivering corrective feedback, great leaders pause and ask a powerful question: *What's actually driving this behavior?* Because while it's easy to assume a performer just "isn't trying," the truth is far more nuanced—and far more fixable.

Sometimes the issue isn't motivation. It's that the performer **can't** do the task fluently yet. Or they **don't** have access to a reliable process. Or maybe the feedback they need has been missing. When leaders misdiagnose performance problems, they not only waste time correcting symptoms—they risk punishing the performer for system failures.

That's where the **Performance Diagnostic Checklist (PDC)** comes in.

The PDC is a behavior-analytic tool developed from decades of research in Organizational Behavior Management (OBM). It helps leaders diagnose the root causes of performance breakdowns across *four key domains*:

1. **Training** – Has the person been trained—and practiced—until fluent?

2. **Task Support** – Are expectations, prompts, and models easily accessible in the environment?

3. **Tools & Processes** – Does the performer have the materials, resources, and time to succeed?

4. **Consequences** – Are effective, timely reinforcers in place to support the behavior?

There is a copy in the Appendix for you to reference. By walking through these categories, leaders can determine whether performance issues stem from **a lack of skill, unclear expectations, ineffective systems,** or **insufficient reinforcement**. Once you know the source, the path forward becomes clear—and feedback becomes not just easier to give, but far more likely to work.

DO THIS → NOT THAT

Most performance issues aren't about motivation—they're about barriers. When leaders jump straight to correction without understanding the root cause, they risk addressing the wrong problem and eroding trust in the process.

That's where the **Performance Diagnostic Checklist** (Carr et al., 2013) comes in. It shifts the focus from blaming the performer to evaluating the conditions around them—training, systems, tools, and consequences. Because if it's a **can't do**, no amount of "try harder" will fix it.

Here's what that looks like in practice: this approach transforms feedback into a precision instrument. Leaders who use the PDC focus on engineering improvement through careful diagnosis before delivering feedback. Diagnosing before delivering increases the likelihood that behavior will stick.

Do This

Use the PDC to assess what's truly driving the behavior—skill, system, or reinforcement?

Example: "Let's run a quick Performance Diagnostic Checklist to see if this is a fluency issue, a system barrier, or something else."

Diagnose whether it's a can't do (skill) or won't do (performance) problem before acting

Example: "Have they been taught how to do this? Or are they choosing not to for another reason?"

Train to fluency first—then expect independent performance

Example: "Before holding them accountable, let's make sure they've practiced with feedback until the skill is fluent."

Provide precise, observable expectations and visible prompts

Example: "During transitions, all students should be in line within 30 seconds, facing forward, and silent."

Target reinforcement toward high-leverage, high-impact behaviors

Example: Reinforcing when staff model new safety protocols under pressure.

Simplify the process, clarify workflows, and remove barriers that block performance
Example: "Let's remove two unnecessary steps from the referral process so staff can complete it during their shift."

Not That

Correct without knowing the root cause
Example: Delivering feedback or consequences without analyzing why the behavior is occurring in the first place.

Assume every gap is a motivation issue
Example: "They're just not trying hard enough."

Deliver feedback to someone who's never been trained
Example: "You should know this by now," when no formal training occurred.

Give vague goals or unclear expectations
Example: "Make sure transitions go more smoothly."

Reinforce everything equally

Example: Saying "great job" to everyone regardless of what behaviors were actually seen.

Ignore system constraints

Example: Expecting consistent documentation when the process is confusing, time-consuming, or glitchy.

SUMMARY

Corrective feedback only works when it targets the right problem. When you deliver it without diagnosis, you risk punishing the wrong thing—or the wrong person.

The most effective leaders give feedback grounded in a deep understanding of behavior. They assess whether the issue relates to ability, clarity, systems, or motivation, and respond appropriately. Use the Performance Diagnostic Checklist as your leadership compass. Effective correction starts with understanding, not assumption.

CHAPTER 12

YOUR FEEDBACK LEGACY

HOW YOU GIVE FEEDBACK TODAY SHAPES THE ORGANIZATION OF TOMORROW

Some leaders leave behind systems. Others leave behind scars. What kind of legacy will your feedback create?

You don't build your feedback legacy in one all-hands meeting, during performance reviews, or through well-crafted mission statements. You build it in the everyday moments—how you respond to effort, how you redirect missteps, and whether you make feedback safe, clear, and reinforcing.

The truth is, your feedback legacy doesn't live in what you *said*. It lives in what they *do* when you're not in the room. It lives in how your people feel about their work. And it lives in the behaviors they pass on to others.

It's not about whether *you* think your feedback was clear, helpful, or motivating. It's about whether it had the intended effect. And whether it cultivated a culture where feedback isn't feared—but sought out, delivered well, and used to grow.

That's the measure of real leadership. That's the feedback legacy.

The Behavioral Indicators

Legacy isn't measured in mission statements or exit interviews. It's measured in behavior—specifically, the patterns that persist when you're no longer the one guiding them. If your feedback isn't shaping performers into more skilled, confident, and self-sufficient contributors, then the system you've built isn't sustainable.

These indicators show whether feedback functions as a system of reinforcement rather than just a habit of telling. They reveal if performers are developing the capacity to deliver, receive, and use feedback effectively, or if they are simply surviving under it. Use these signals to assess the health of your feedback ecosystem.

Leader Behavior:

- Fails to seek feedback from team members

  Example: A manager rolls out a new process and closes the meeting with "Any questions?" followed by silence. They take the silence as agreement rather than discomfort. Over time, gaps in the process persist, and resentment builds—unspoken but active.

- Assumes feedback is understood because "no one said otherwise"

  Example: After a one-time coaching conversation, a supervisor never revisits the topic. When the issue resurfaces, they express frustration: "I already talked to you about this." The performer, unsure of expectations, stopped trying to guess what the feedback meant.

- Doesn't assess the long-term impact of their feedback on performance

  Example: A team lead gives positive feedback after a presentation: "Nice job!" Weeks later, the same errors reappear. Because no specific behavior was reinforced, no behavior changed—just good feelings that faded fast.

- Keeps the feedback loop hierarchical—only flowing top-down

  Example: During meetings, a leader critiques team performance but never asks for input on their own leadership. The result? A lopsided loop where staff feel managed—but not mentored. Leadership is perceived as untouchable.

- Avoids giving feedback altogether to avoid conflict

  Example: A supervisor sees a consistent drop in productivity from one team member but chooses not to say anything "because they've been stressed lately." The behavior becomes normalized—not addressed—reinforcing silence over support.

Performer Behavior:

- Struggles to describe what high performance looks like in their role

  Example: When asked what excellence looks like, a frontline employee says, "Just not getting in trouble, I guess." Without clear, reinforced standards, the performer aims for avoidance—not achievement.

- Gives generic feedback to peers, if at all

  Example: A staff member tells a colleague, "Good work," without specifying what was done well. Even well-meaning praise becomes noise when it lacks contingency and clarity.

- Avoids speaking up about unclear expectations

  Example: A team member doesn't understand the new workflow but nods along in meetings. In private, they admit, "I didn't want to look dumb." Fear of judgment overrides the pursuit of clarity.

- Relies on formal reviews instead of day-to-day guidance

  Example: An employee says, "I guess I'll find out if I'm doing okay during my evaluation." In the absence of ongoing feedback, performance becomes guesswork—and growth stalls.

- Fails to reinforce others—even when noticing great performance

  Example: A team member sees a colleague handle a difficult client call with grace. They think, "That was impressive," but say nothing. Without modeling or prompting, reinforcement remains private—and behavior change stays unlikely.

Together, these behaviors paint a picture of a system stuck in neutral. Feedback may be occurring, but it's not *functional*. And when feedback fails to shape behavior or build capacity, it becomes a missed opportunity as opposed to a meaningful legacy.

The Behavioral Solution

If feedback isn't producing more confident, capable performers, then it's not leadership—it's lip service. Legacy, in behavioral terms, is about **generalization and maintenance**. *In short, are people able to do the right things across situations—and keep doing them over time—even when you're not around?* Can they coach and reinforce each other's behavior because you've modeled and shaped that behavior in them?

The goal is to create better performance by building a feedback-rich culture that endures beyond your direct involvement. This culture reinforces excellence, learning, and psychological safety through the contingencies you establish.

That's not a feel-good idea—it's a measurable, observable system. And behavior science gives us the blueprint to build it.

To create a legacy that empowers others to do the same, leaders must build systems where feedback:

- Is delivered **regularly** and **precisely**
- Reinforces the **right behaviors**, not just outcomes
- Builds **fluency** in others—not just compliance
- Encourages **two-way flow**, not one-way direction

To leave a feedback legacy, you need more than well-intentioned conversations—you need systems that outlast your presence and empower others to lead well when you're not in the room. That kind of legacy isn't built on charisma or clever slogans. It's built on contingencies that shape behavior and feedback loops that are functional, fluent, and reciprocal.

When feedback becomes part of the operating system—not just a tool used during reviews or crises—you're no longer just managing people. You're shaping a culture of reinforcement. One where people learn not only how to perform, but how to support performance in others.

To build that kind of culture and legacy, leaders must:

- **Model it**

  Example: A leader consistently gives feedback using behavior-specific praise—"I appreciated how you stayed calm and asked clarifying questions during that escalation call"—and over time, their team starts using the same style when recognizing each other.

- **Teach it**

  Example: During onboarding, team leads walk new hires through how to give and receive feedback effectively, including practice scenarios. They reinforce attempts and correct missteps—ensuring fluency in both giving and receiving.

- **Systematize it**

  Example: The organization builds a short feedback block into all meetings—15 seconds for wins, 30 seconds for course corrections. Over time, feedback becomes just another part of how the team communicates—not something awkward or rare.

- **Check the impact**

  Example: A department head tracks whether key behaviors (e.g., proactive communication, error-checking) are improving after feedback cycles. If not, they adjust the feedback format—adding more modeling or shifting timing—to improve effectiveness.

- **Get social validity**

  Example: After performance conversations, a leader follows up: "Was that helpful? Anything you wish I'd done differently?" Over time, the team gets better at giving feedback on the feedback. The leader doesn't rely on silence as approval—they verify whether the impact matched the intention.

DO THIS → NOT THAT

Even well-meaning leaders can fall into patterns that feel efficient but fail to reinforce—or worse, inadvertently punish—the very behaviors they want more of. When feedback isn't deliberate, it becomes noise. When it's generic, it becomes forgettable. And when it's unexamined, it becomes a liability. The fix isn't to do more—it's to do better. That means shifting from habit to intention, from assumptions to data, and from charisma to contingencies. To lead more effectively, replace these common habits with behaviorally sound practices. Do this—not that:

Do This

Actively solicit input to evaluate feedback effectiveness

Example: "How's the feedback you've been getting lately? Anything we should do differently to make it more useful?"

Use daily, observable behaviors as feedback data

Example: "I've noticed you're following up with clients within the same day—that consistency is making a real difference."

Adapt feedback to performer needs and roles

Example: Giving more frequent check-ins to new team members, and high-level strategy feedback to experienced staff.

Tie recognition to specific, reinforcing contingencies

Example: "You stepping in to cover that shift helped us stay fully staffed—that kind of support keeps our system running."

Recognize it's about the systems and behaviors you leave behind

Example: "If I'm not here, will people still know what good performance looks like and how to reinforce it?"

Not That

Assume no complaints means success

Example: No one's pushing back or speaking up—so you assume everything's fine.

Wait for annual reviews to assess performance

Example: Holding off on meaningful feedback until a scheduled performance evaluation.

Give the same feedback to everyone

Example: Telling every team member "just keep it up," regardless of their performance or goals.

Think praise alone drives performance

Example: Saying "Thanks for your hard work!" without connecting it to what mattered.

Believe leadership legacy is about results alone

Example: Measuring success only by data or outcomes, not the sustainability of the culture or practices you helped shape.

Your Feedback Footprint: What Will They Say When You're Gone?

In the end, your feedback legacy will be measured by the culture you cultivated. Did you create more people who know how to shape behavior—ethically, skillfully, and effectively? Or did people spend their time guessing what you wanted, fearing your corrections, or faking their way through your praise?

If your leadership disappeared tomorrow, what would stay behind?

- Would feedback still flow?
- Would behavior still improve?
- Would the culture still reinforce excellence?

Building that kind of legacy requires behavioral precision, care, and consistency. This approach goes beyond traditional leadership as it creates true leverage. Start now. Shape the culture. Build the systems. Reinforce the behaviors. Leave behind something greater than your name.

REFERENCES

Alvero, A. M., Bucklin, B. R., & Austin, J. (2001). An objective review of the effectiveness and essential characteristics of performance feedback in organizational settings (1985–1998). *Journal of Organizational Behavior Management, 21(1)*, 3–29.

Carr JE, Wilder DA, Majdalany L, Mathisen D, Strain LA. An Assessment-based Solution to a Human-Service Employee Performance Problem: An Initial Evaluation of the Performance Diagnostic Checklist - Human Services. *Behav Anal Pract. 2013 Spring;6(1)*:16-32. doi: 10.1007/BF03391789. PMID: 25729505; PMCID: PMC3680147.

Gallup. (2019, October 16). *Feedback is not enough.* Gallup. https://www.gallup.com/workplace/257582/feedback-not-enough.aspx

Gallup & Workhuman. (2023, June 12). *Organizations need to redefine feedback -- and include recognition.* Gallup. https://www.gallup.com/workplace/651812/organizations-redefine-feedback-including-recognition.aspx

Mangiapanello, K. A., & Hemmes, N. S. (2015). *An analysis of feedback from a behavior analytic perspective. The Behavior Analyst,* 38(1), 51–75. https://doi.org/10.1007/s40614-014-0026-x

APPENDIX

Performance Diagnostic Checklist (PDC)

Use this checklist before delivering corrective feedback to ensure you've identified the true root cause of performance gaps.

1. Training

Has the performer received adequate training for the task?

- ☐ Has the performer been trained on the task expectations?
- ☐ Has the performer demonstrated the skill accurately during training?
- ☐ Has the performer had enough practice to reach fluency (speed + accuracy)?
- ☐ Was feedback provided during training to shape performance?
- ☐ Has the skill been practiced under natural conditions, not just simulations?

2. Task Support

Is the environment structured to cue the right behavior?

- ☐ Are task expectations clearly communicated and documented?
- ☐ Are prompts or job aids (e.g., checklists, visuals) available and accessible?
- ☐ Is there a clear performance standard (e.g., what good looks like)?
- ☐ Are goals or deadlines provided in advance?
- ☐ Is help available when needed?

3. Tools & Processes

Does the performer have the materials and systems to succeed?

- ☐ Are necessary tools or materials available and functional?
- ☐ Are procedures streamlined and not overly complex?
- ☐ Are competing tasks prioritized or scheduled logically?
- ☐ Is the physical environment free from unnecessary distractions or barriers?
- ☐ Are workflows and systems designed to support the behavior?

4. Consequences

Are desired behaviors reinforced in a timely and meaningful way?

- ☐ Are positive consequences delivered immediately following desired behavior?
- ☐ Does the performer receive regular feedback on performance?
- ☐ Are outcomes meaningful and aligned with the performer's values?
- ☐ Is undesirable behavior being inadvertently reinforced?
- ☐ Are performers recognized for consistent effort, not just results?

Tip:

If you check **one or more boxes** in any category as "**No**", address those issues before providing corrective feedback. Performance problems are often the result of **systems, skills,** or **supports—** not just motivation.

ABOUT THE AUTHOR

Paul "Paulie" Gavoni, Ed.D., BCBA-D

Heartscienceinternational.org

Dr. Paul "Paulie" Gavoni has been called the most prolific disseminator of behavior analysis in modern history—reaching millions each year through his books, top-ranked podcasts, and viral content. A globally recognized thought leader and Wall Street Journal and USA Today best-selling author, Paulie is known for blending the science of behavior with straight-shooting strategies that drive performance and lasting change.

From education and human services to combat sports, he applies **Organizational Behavior Management (OBM)** to help people and systems thrive. In combat sports, he's known as Coach Paulie Gloves—a former Golden Gloves Heavyweight Champion who has developed local, state, national, and world champion fighters using the same science that transforms classrooms and companies.

As the founder of **Heart & Science International** and co-founder of **The Behavioral Toolbox**, Paulie delivers practical, science-based solutions for real-world problems. His leadership roles—including COO, professor, and school turnaround manager—reflect decades of experience helping individuals and organizations perform at their best.

A board member for the **World Behavior Analysis Day Alliance**, Paulie continues to lead global efforts to expand the reach and relevance of behavioral science. Whether working with educators, clinicians, executives, or athletes, he is known for his authenticity, humor, and results-driven philosophy: integrity, growth, and real change through the science of human behavior.

Books by the Author

If *The Feedback Effect: Lead Smarter, Not Harder With the Science of Human Behavior* resonated with you, check out these other titles grounded in the science of human behavior and designed to create meaningful impact:

Positional Authority Ain't Leadership

In a sea of leadership theories and styles, *Positional Authority Ain't Leadership* stands out as a beacon, guiding readers to understand that the essence of true leadership lies in the principles of behavioral analysis. This book offers more than just theories; it provides a scientific approach to leadership, making it a unique and essential read.

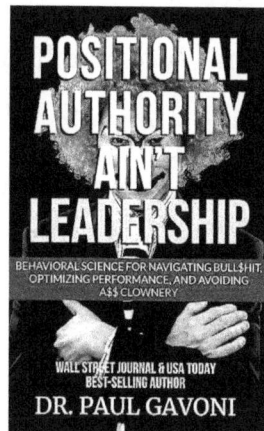

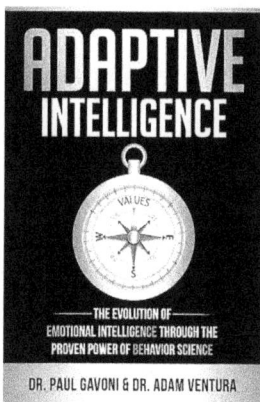

Adaptive Intelligence (*co-authored with Dr. Adam Ventura*)

Adaptive Intelligence builds on the foundation of emotional intelligence by going deeper—focusing not just on emotions, but on understanding *why* we and others do the things we do, and *why* we often fail to take effective action when it's needed. Grounded in the science of behavior and evolutionary theory, *Adaptive Intelligence* provides a practical, evidence-based framework for aligning behavior with core values, overcoming obstacles, creating lasting change, and producing measurable results.

Finding Your Authentic Self

Ever feel like you're doing everything right, but something still feels off? *Finding Your Authentic Self* helps you close the gap between how you're living and who you really are. Grounded in the science of human behavior, this book gives you practical tools to identify your values, examine your patterns, and build habits that reflect the life you want—not the one you've settled for. You'll learn how to stop drifting, start choosing, and take action that aligns with your core. Whether you're leading others or trying to lead yourself, this book gives you a clear process for showing up with purpose and building a life you can be proud of—one behavior at a time.

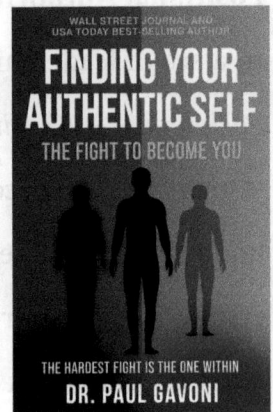

Connect with the Author

To learn more about Dr. Gavoni's keynotes, training, and coaching services, visit Heartscienceinternational.org

HEART & SCIENCE
International

Lead Smarter, Not Harder

Leadership isn't about doing more—it's about doing what matters.

Leadership Training

We help leaders lead with purpose—not just position. Our trainings are grounded in the science of behavior and designed to align leadership actions with organizational values and outcomes. Using our Four Hats model, we build leadership fluency at every level.

Leadership Coaching

Our coaching turns goals into measurable results. We align key performance indicators with observable behaviors, use diagnostics to remove barriers, and apply proven OBM strategies to engineer sustainable performance improvement.

Performance Engineering

We don't just launch change—we build values-based systems to sustain it. From Behavior Systems Analysis and performance engineering to coach-the-coach support, we help teams design environments that positively influence behavior toward desired results.

Keynotes & Presentations

We deliver keynotes that move people—from insight to action. Popular topics include Adaptive Intelligence, Positional Authority Ain't Leadership, Quick Wins, and Deliberate Coaching. Each session blends science, storytelling, and humor to inspire reflection and change.

In every organization, results require behavior.

The true measure of a leader is found in the behavior of their people. When you get the right behaviors moving in the right direction, the right results follow. The Four Hats of Leadership are grounded in the science of human behavior—built to develop and sustain performance at the individual, team, and organizational levels.

The Four Hats of Leadership

- Leading
- Training
- Coaching
- Managing

**Leadership sparks the fire.
Management keeps it burning.**

thedeliberatecoach@gmail.com

Paul "Paulie" Gavoni, Ed.D. BCBA-D

www.heartscienceinternational.org